Home Front

Life in the towns and villages of Bromley in the Great War

Edited by Christine Hellicar

First published in 2014
by
BBLHS Publications
150 Worlds End Lane, Chelsfield, BR6 6AS
www.bblhs.org.uk
admin@bblhs.org.uk

ISBN 978-0-9574633-1-8

Printed by Russell Press, www.russellpress.com

Bromley Borough Local History Society

Formed in 1974, the Bromley Borough Local History Society gives those with an interest in the history of any part of the borough a chance to meet, to exchange information and learn more about the borough's history.

Its members help preserve records and carry out research, which is published in print and online, on a wide range of topics and places.

In co-operation with the Local Studies Library, museums and other organisations, we make sure at least some of our history is preserved for future generations.

The society covers all areas within the present-day London Borough of Bromley:

Anerley - Beckenham - Bickley -Biggin Hill
Bromley - Chelsfield - Chislehurst - Coney Hall
Cudham - Downe - Farnborough - Green Street Green
Hayes - Keston - Leaves Green - Mottingham
Orpington - Penge - Petts Wood - St Mary Cray
St Paul's Cray - Shortlands - Sundridge Park
West Wickham.

www.bblhs.org.uk

Contents

Acknowledgements

Many people have contributed to this book. Some have a family connection with Bromley borough going back generations, others are newcomers who have found themselves fascinated by the rich history of their chosen home. They are not professional historians. They come from all walks of life: teachers, administrators, scientists, journalists etc, who share an interest in researching and writing about local history.

Each chapter has been written by a different person, reflecting their personal interest or experience, and all are, or have been, members of Bromley Borough Local History Society.

The author of each main article is named and the editor is the writer of uncredited material. Many Society members have contributed their time to research, write, proof read and provide information from their collections including Elaine Baker, Joanna Friel, David Johnson, Pat Manning, Paul Rason, Michael Rawcliffe, Val Stealey, Cliff Watkins and Jean Wilson. I thank them for all their help and offer my apologies to anyone I have missed out.

The staff at Bromley Local Studies Library have assisted me and others in sourcing pictures from the archive and tracking down original material.

Last, but not least, I have had the invaluable support and encouragement of my husband Patrick as well as his practical and professional expertise in the production of this book.

Photographs are credited on page or are from the following collections:

Bromley Local Studies Library (BLSL)
Alan Cheesman (AC)
Ron Cox (RC)
Joanna Friel, Chislehurst Society (JF)
Peter Heinecke (PH)
Christine Hellicar (CH)
Frans Van Humbeek (FVH)
Peter Leigh (PL)
David Johnson (DJ)
Steve Miller (SM)
Orpington History Organisation (OHO)
Michael Rawcliffe (MR)
Jean Wilson (JW)

Christine Hellicar, 2014

Chislehurst Lads Leaving For The Front, July 10th 1915.

As the lads left for the front, *their families and friends were there to cheer them on their way. The soldiers pictured here, and on the front cover, were photographed in Chislehurst in 1915. (BLSL)*

Introduction

Michael Rawcliffe and Christine Hellicar

This book is not a history of the First World War. It is not even a history of what is now the London Borough of Bromley — a collection of small towns and villages — during the First World War. It is a series of snapshots, in words and pictures, which capture how this momentous event affected people and places.

Many articles focus on a specific location in the borough and a different aspect of wartime life. We look at town and village life, the work of the Red Cross, industry and farming and discover how people's day-to-day existence changed.

These people lived in a world at war, but they also lived in a very different Bromley from the one we know today. The present London Borough of Bromley is the largest of the 32 London boroughs and also one of the most geographically diverse. In the northern half of the borough, Penge, Beckenham, Bromley, Chislehurst, Orpington, Hayes and West Wickham are suburbs with many commuters and a high-density population. To the south the borough extends to the North Downs with a largely rural population in the numerous villages and hamlets which have retained much of their early 20th century character.

In 1914 the urban areas such as Bromley were smaller and many of today's suburbs were still

Population figures for towns and villages of Bromley from the 1921 census

	Men	Women	Total
Bromley	15,264	19,788	35,052
Beckenham	14,169	19,176	33,345
Penge	11,892	14,312	26,284
Chislehurst	3,947	5,034	8,981
Orpington	3,700	3,347	7,047
Farnborough [1]	1,643	1,679	3,322
Cudham	1,141	1,106	2,247
St Mary Cray	1,016	1,162	2,178
Chelsfield	979	1,129	2,108
Mottingham	892	912	1,804
St Paul's Cray	708	804	1,512
West Wickham	594	707	1,301
Keston	489	540	1,029
Hayes	364	646	1,010
Downe	323	468	791

Census of England and Wales: County of Kent 1921 HMSO 1923
[1] Farnborough contained the Union Workhouse on the site of the present Princess Royal University Hospital

villages. Bromley town was the only municipal borough within the boundaries of the present London Borough. Beckenham, Chislehurst and Orpington still had Urban District Councils. Together, these four had the other villages as civil parishes under their jurisdiction.

The census is carried out every 10 years and the figures given on the opposite page are from the 1921 census when the total population of the borough was under 150,000, less than half the current figure. Only three areas had population greater than 10,000 — Beckenham, Bromley and Penge. West Wickham and Hayes were still villages.

In virtually all the census areas in 1921 there were more women than men. But this was not merely because so many men died in the war. In the growing suburban areas in particular, women already outnumbered men before 1914 because of the large numbers, often from the local villages, in domestic service. Some worked as "maids of all work", being the only servant in the house. But the prosperous households in areas such as Bickley had a range of specialist servants such as cooks, ladies' maids, butlers and gardeners. Think Downton Abbey on a smaller scale.

Some people — those with the servants — commuted to the City of London but most people lived and shopped where they worked and many, particularly women and children, only occasionally ventured beyond their village or town boundaries.

Telephones were virtually unheard of and communication was by letter and postcard or, for urgent news, telegram. The train network was as extensive as today's but on the road horse-drawn transport was more common than motorised and many roads were still unmade.

War memorials with their names of the fallen bring home to us the numbers killed in the war and how the smallest hamlet was affected. In addition to civic war memorials, many occupations, from the Post Office to factories, lost workers and many were to remember their sacrifice by plaques at their place of work. These memorials bear witness today to the big change the war brought, but right from the outbreak of war life changed, not just for the soldiers but those left behind.

Change began in August 1914 when a patriotic fever gripped the nation, and Bromley was no different. Hundreds of young men volunteered and usually joined their local regiment, but not enough. In 1916 conscription was introduced. Now older men and those whose jobs were important at home — such as agricultural workers — were going to the front. Those who claimed to be pacifists had to go before a tribunal to prove their case. If successful they were sent to do essential work in industries such as coal mining. Those who were exempt due to poor health, were often accused of cowardice and taunted by being given a white feather. Many took to wearing badges showing that they were engaged in essential work at home.

Kent was the closest English county to the Western

Front and by September 1914 trains were bringing the wounded to hospitals here and in the other Home Counties. Some large houses were requisitioned as temporary hospitals, as were public buildings such as Orpington Village Hall and the newly-built Balgowan School in Beckenham, which became a hospital for the returning wounded before it was used as a school.

As the wounded became more mobile, they were able to go out into the community and were given distinctive civilian clothing so they could be recognised as war wounded and not malingerers.

Women volunteered as nurses in dozens of makeshift hospitals and Orpington housed many wounded Commonwealth soldiers in a special hospital built by the Canadians — a hospital whose modern replacement on the same site still serves the people of Orpington today.

When the men left for the front, many vacancies were filled by women and their contribution to the war effort was in part responsible for those over the age of 30 being given the vote after the war. As the war years dragged on all parts of the community were affected: wives lost husbands, children fathers, there were food and transport shortages and people struggled to cope with everyday life.

It is these changes that are reflected in this book, which is the result of research drawing on rich and varied local historical sources. At the end of the book there is a sources guide to help those who might wish to do further research.

The Drill Hall *in Bromley's East Street,
on the right in this picture. It was from
here that the Kent Territorials left for a
training camp in July 1914. By the time
they returned war had been declared and
they were heading for the Western Front.
The Drill Hall still stands today but is now
a pub and restaurant. The tower of the old
town hall in Bromley Market Square can
be seen in the background. (BBLHS)*

Calm Before the Storm

Max Batten

Life across Bromley as reflected in the local newspapers in the days just before and after the outbreak of the First World War

What turned out to be the first shots of the Great War were fired when Austria attacked Serbia on 28 July 1914, but three days later local papers had not fully caught-up. Unless you understood the various rivalries and treaties that existed the assassination of the heir to the Austria-Hungary throne a month before was not seen by the average citizen as of much note, although it is equally clear that some people were aware of "problems" in Europe. By the time of the next issue of the papers, however, the country was at war and significant changes were beginning to appear.

Last week of July — peace

At the end of July 1914, for the first time, the annual training camp of the Kent Territorials was taking place in Hampshire. A and B Companies of the 5th Battalion (Royal West Kent Regiment) left the Drill Hall in East Street to join a special noon train from Bromley South. The 110 men, led by Captain Hay, were accompanied to the station by a band and many friends and well-wishers as they started their rather tortuous journey to Liphook via Tonbridge. They were due to complete their march to Salisbury Plain on 3 August. The Beckenham and Penge Company were more fortunate, entraining at Kent House at 12.28pm, travelling via Wimbledon and arriving around four o'clock.

Perhaps many of them had been to Crystal Palace on Saturday 25 July to see the last in a series of military tattoos. The park was well used in those days and there was to be a series of grand firework displays every Thursday during August and on the Bank Holiday Monday, 3 August. Among many other events over the Bank Holiday, William Cook opened his poultry farm to visitors, just two minutes from Orpington station. At the West Chislehurst

Football *attracted large crowds. Many of the spectators pictured above at the Crystal Palace v Hove match in 1914 would have been in the trenches within months (MR)*

An organised swimming club *met at Keston ponds, below, between 1910 and 1919. They used the middle pond and installed a diving board. Informal swimming continued into the 1930s. A correspondent to the* Chislehurst Times *in July 1914 was concerned there was no lifeboat. Eventually there was a fatality and the local authority then introduced a by-law banning swimming. (BLSL)*

Dairy Farm, there were more than 500 entries for the sports and gala, including what proved to be a controversial five-mile race where, on a circular track, it became difficult to count accurately the number of laps completed by each contestant! However, the winner of the bicycle musical chairs rode away with half a ton of coal as his prize, the music being provided by the Brixton and Clapham Silver Band, and £70 was raised for local charities.

On the cricket field, with plenty of matches in the district during the week, one in particular stood out when Eltham visited Grove Park, who held out for a draw despite Dr WG Grace scoring 69 not out and taking four wickets. In the summer weather there was much activity at Keston Ponds with swimming, diving, racing and polo. A correspondent to the *Chislehurst Times* was concerned, however, at the lack of a life-saving boat.

On 27 July, Miss Starling had addressed a meeting of the Conservative and Unionist Women's Franchise Association at Scadbury on the question of votes for women and the advantages and benefits this would bring. *The Beckenham Journal*, however, was more concerned with "Solving the Servant Problem" by bringing "mistress and maid together". This advert continued into the post-start-of-war edition, so obviously someone had not appreciated it was going to get very much worse!

In Chislehurst where, because of failing eyesight, Miss Owen had recently retired as headmistress of St Nicholas School after 41 years in the profession, a grateful community had raised enough money to buy her a supplementary annuity of £10-12s-0d [£10.60]. Speech Day at St Hugh's School on 29 July went well, with the Hon Dudley Gordon (second son of the Earl of Aberdeen) giving "a manly address to the boys". On the same day, at Springhill in Bromley, prizes were being awarded at the County School for Domestic Economy. Much praise was heaped upon these "home makers of the future" who had, among other useful skills, learnt how to provide a cheap dinner for seven persons.

At St Paul's Cray paper works a strike by workers over low pay and lack of union recognition was entering its fourth week with clashes between strikers and the police. A rumour that men "conveyed by motor" had been seen entering the works led to an

Daylight Saving — *putting the clocks forward an hour in the spring each year and back again in the autumn — was introduced in 1916.*

The emergency law was brought in to reduce energy consumption and increase war production. It became permanent following the passing of the 1925 Summer Time Act.

But it was 20 years earlier in 1905 that the idea occurred to Chislehurst builder William Willett, pictured right. On his early morning rides across Chislehurst Commons Willett saw shutters and blinds closed well after the sun had risen in spring and summer and in the spring the evenings were dark relatively early, so that the warmer evenings were wasted.

Willett came up with the solution of daylight saving and wrote a pamphlet, The Waste of Daylight. *Despite having many supporters, including the young Winston Churchill, Willett's idea was rejected. It took war with Germany to persuade the Government to adopt his proposal.*

William Willett did not live to see his idea enacted as he died aged 58, from influenza, in 1915. A blue plaque on the wall of his house, The Cedars *in Camden Park Road, a road name in Petts Wood —* Willett Way *— and a sundial memorial in Willett Wood, pictured above, commemorate William Willett and his grand idea.*

Source: David Prerau, www.savingthedaylight.com
chislehurst-society.org.uk (JF)

increase in the number of policemen and pickets at the gates. On Wednesday 29 July a parade of strikers marched through St Paul's Cray and St Mary Cray, led by a band. Only the coming of war finally led to the dispute being settled on 5 August.

In Beckenham, the Urban District Council at their meeting on 27 July were more exercised by complaints from residents of Manor Road about motor traffic nuisance (the 10mph warning boards were being ignored), a recent fatality and litter being left by newspaper boys on the Cator Estate. The local paper commented on the pace of change in Beckenham High Street, with the construction of a new cinema theatre and the closure of the "quaint old milk shop at No 85". It agreed that much work needed to be done on local roads but praised the school authorities at St Johns in Penge who had released some land from their playground to improve the junction at Croydon Road.

Speeding traffic was a regular cause of court appearances in Bromley. At the end of July, Henry March from Bexley was fined 30 shillings (£1.50p) for exceeding 20mph (accused of doing 29, he admitted to 24½) while a 63 year-old lady from Chelsea received a similar fine for doing 29mph on Bromley Common. A motor-cyclist from Richmond, caught at the same spot and on an unregistered bike, was alleged to be travelling at 38mph. Even a bus driver was fined 10 shillings(50p) for exceeding by 5mph the 12mph limit set for his vehicle on Main Road in Sidcup.

Bromley Rural District Council (RDC), chaired by Sir Henry Lennard, were concerned about smells and "the bellowing day and night" from Mr Shipps' slaughterhouse in St Mary Cray High Street, near Mill Bridge. It was decided to review his licence when it came up for renewal in December. They had to deal also with a complaint from Mr William Willett (see opposite page) of The Cedars, Chislehurst, about the obstruction of a bridle path from St Mary Cray gasworks past Mr Nash's farm to Foots Cray. Additionally, a letter from Mr H Golding complained about his neighbour watering his garden from his cess pool, making it impossible for Mr Golding to sit out or even leave a window open. A promise from the neighbour not to do it "more than necessary" had been received and apparently accepted as resolution of the case. More seriously, Walter Wood, who owned premises at Hayesford, had "allowed" his cess pool to overflow into the River Ravensbourne and received a 20 shilling (£1) fine.

Orpington Parish Council had looked into provision of a recreation ground, approved a new hall for All Saints Parish Church and received a report from the medical officer. He advised that a case of diphtheria had been reported, along with two cases of scarlet fever, and that measles had been reported among the fruit-pickers at Ramsden, but "fortunately" they had now left the area.

At the busy Bromley Police Court, a young domestic, Eva Workman, was facing charges of stealing cash (subsequently found hidden in her stockings) and valuables (found in her room). Richard Head, aged 62, was charged with disorderly conduct and using obscene language at the George and Dragon in Farnborough. He had fortunately failed to kick a policeman (after

The Cray Valley was one of the most important fruit growing areas of Kent and travellers, pictured here at St Mary Cray, would come each summer to pick the fruit that was destined for the London market. But there was little sympathy when travellers' children were afflicted by an outbreak of measles (CH)

several tries) but was fined 15 shillings (75p) with five shillings (25p) costs. An unlicensed pedlar, William Cunningham, found in Farnborough, was luckier: he got off with a caution. Penge Police Court also had five cases of drunk and disorderly to deal with on 27 July alone. Regrettably, one of those found guilty admitted he was a stranger to the district (being from Bermondsey) and rightly the Clerk pointed out: "That is all the more reason why you should behave yourself when you come to Penge." He was fined 2s-6d [12½p] plus costs 4s-6d [22½p]

Moral outrage was caused when, in front of magistrate Mr Thomas Dewey, 34 year-old Alfred Mitchell was sentenced to 21 days hard labour for leaving his three children — aged eight, six and three — in the workhouse while earning 24 shillings (£1.20p) a week on a Sidcup farm. While he argued that he could not both work and child-mind, the newspaper headline made the situation clear: "Not fair to ratepayers"!

Further afield, at the offices of the Official Receiver in Westminster, the former owner of the George Hotel in Hayes was attending the first meeting of his creditors. His debts of £487-15s-6d were not matched by his assets of £10. Happily for him, such other property that he still had in Catford apparently belonged to his wife!

Less contentiously, *The Bromley Times* published an advert by the Bromley and Beckenham Joint Hospital Board for a new building for bedrooms for nurses at the Hospital for Infectious Diseases at Skym Corner on Bromley Common. However, at a meeting of the Hospital Board, the cost of maintaining 28 "County" patients, at 35 shillings [£1.75] a week was getting too much and it was resolved that the Kent Insurance Committee (KIC) must either clear the debt or remove its patients. The KIC had already agreed to pay travelling expenses to persons attending tuberculosis dispensaries from country districts, so the outlook was hopeful.

A letter from Councillor William Gibbs of 36 Hammelton Road in Bromley was asking for help in providing 850 small bunches of flowers for the annual visit he arranged for men and women from the poorest parts of east and south London "who did not have the privilege of living in Bromley". A free dinner and tea would be provided in the nearby Central Hall in London Road.

The *Beckenham Journal*, perhaps short of local news, took a less parochial attitude than its Bromley counterpart and included some national and international items. Reporting on 1 August that a state of war existed between Austria-Hungary and Serbia. It added that the long-serving Foreign Secretary Sir Edward Grey was trying to keep the other Powers out of the dispute. Nevertheless, the Navy was already moving some vessels to new positions.

By Sunday 2 August, some at least were becoming aware of dark days ahead and, on page two of the following Friday's *Bromley & District Times* (the front page was always filled with advertisements), a long paragraph headed "The Shadow of War" was given prominence, being a verbatim report of the sermon given by Rev Knight at St Mary's Shortlands, who had scrapped his planned exhortation to muse instead on "... how paradoxical it seems to be! A shot fired by a madman has set Europe in turmoil."

However, Cudham's third annual Fete and Fair had gone ahead as planned on Saturday and Monday at Westerham Hill, including the Baby Show. Money raised from the event was to go towards the provision of a resident, trained nurse in the village. And on Monday, at Sundridge Park, a large crowd had attended Bromley's 11th Charter Day commemoration, with lots of sports, a horse parade and flower show with music from the Blackbird Minstrels and concluding with Mr Brock's fireworks. Entertainment included a tug-of-war, won by Beckenham Police, and the clearly popular musical-chairs on bicycles. Prizes were awarded by Charter Mayor Thomas Dewey with the profits going to Bromley Cottage and PhillipsMemorial hospitals.

The first week of August — war

But things were happening at home — and not all to the good. A letter from the Mayor of Bromley, W Lindley Jones dated Wednesday 5 August was urging people not to panic. Britain had declared war on Germany the previous day. Reports had reached him of "fathers" withdrawing their money from banks (and this must have been the previous week because the Bank Holiday — in its original sense — had been extended to Thursday) and "mothers" purchasing large quantities of stores, which was not fair to the less well-off and aggravated the situation. He had also heard of tradesman raising their prices, which he condemned most strongly. Clearly there had been hoarding, at least by the "gentry", as "A Working Man" complained to the *Beckenham Journal*. It reported one lady, having placed a very large order, wanted it on sale or return in case the war was soon over.

> '*A shot fired by a madman has set Europe in turmoil*'
> — **Rev Knight, St Mary's, Shortlands**

More practically, the chairman of Beckenham Council suggested that allotments be extended and people with large gardens encouraged to grow food, a view advocated by letter-writers such as Miss Edelmann FRHS of Hawkhurst, Chislehurst, among others.

Banks reopened on Friday 7 August and with the Bank Rate reduced to 6%, Chancellor of the Exchequer David Lloyd George confirmed there was "plenty of gold in the country". The Treasury (not the Bank of England) also started printing £1 and 10 shilling [50p] notes, to reduce and replace demand for gold coins (sovereigns and half sovereigns) which the newspaper praised as a sensible precaution. In addition, Postal Orders would also become legal tender. It was with some pride that the *Chislehurst Times* announced that the new banknote paper would be produced at William Joynson and Son's mill in St Mary Cray.

Dr JH Yolland, Kent County Director of the Red Cross, wrote to say hospitals were being prepared to receive the wounded and there was a need for nurses (women) and stretcher bearers (men) together with a request for people to offer their houses for convalescents. This is interesting because, even at this early stage, significant casualties were being anticipated, by some at least. Bromley Red Cross nurses were asked to "see to their surgical appliances" in anticipation of being mobilised, with at least 10 members being needed for foreign service. Local commandant, Miss Coad, based at 61 Masons Hill, was appealing for clothes,

Three days after war was declared *these horses, which the army had commandeered, were pictured outside a Chislehurst Cord Dealers. Motorised transport was also requisitioned, which may have pleased those who the local papers recorded as being exercised by the breaking of the 20mph speed limit. The cars and bus below were pictured at the northern end of Farnborough around 1910. (BLSL and CH)*

sheets and similar items. By coincidence, the previous week had seen the Red Cross summer camp at Rolvenden with more than 200 nurses, including many from the Bromley area, practising dealing with casualties in emergency situations. (See picture P89)

Joan, Lady Camden (writing from Bayham Abbey, Lamberhurst) appealed for funds for the Soldiers' and Sailors' Families Association, to be sent to her or to Coles Child at Bromley Palace. His wife, Clarrie Child, also made an appeal for help, the Association having representatives in all parts of what is now the London Borough of Bromley. More alarmingly, the Chief Scout (Sir Robert Baden-Powell) who had been planning a trip to South Africa to inspect scouts there, had wired from his home in East Sussex to request boys and young men be found to help "guard culverts and telegraphs against spies", provided exemption from school or work was granted.

However, his alarm was clearly not unique, as Beckenham Council had arranged for their Electric Light Station to be illuminated at night and patrolled by a man with a gun with instructions to shoot any suspicious looking characters. "Local gentlemen" in Orpington took it upon themselves to guard the railway bridge there, at least on 4-5 August, and managed to stop an actual suspicious looking individual who was searched and found to be carrying two sausages and a piece of bread in his pockets. More officially, the newspaper had a paragraph headed "Your King and Country Need You" urging all young, unmarried men aged 18 to 30 to rally round the Flag and enlist in the Army immediately. Also, the Mayor was making the Mayor's Parlour in the Town Hall into a registration office for anyone to put their name down as willing to volunteer in whatever activity was required.

It appears Bromley was abuzz with speculation about what was to happen, not least that people would be called up for six months' service. With most of the local Reserves and Territorials on exercises near Salisbury, or in the case of the Kent Cyclist Battalion (which had Bromley and Beckenham detachments), at Broadstairs, there was concern about their return. It transpired that the former had had a very difficult time, being obliged to sleep in ditches with only blankets to keep off the rain while having a long wait for a train home.

Most military activity was centred around the East Street Drill Hall from where troops were leaving at regular intervals even on the first day of war, Wednesday 4 August. Beckenham troops arrived, having marched from Penge Drill Hall, accompanied by many cheers and waving of flags. A large contingent set off by train for Maidstone, the final group passing by the Town Hall to hear encouraging words from the Mayor and accompanied by a large crowd and the inevitable band. A slight anti-climax occurred on Thursday when some Yeomanry (the Reserves) returned for more horses, their own having been commandeered by Regular forces.

It is clear that transport was a major concern. Right from the start horses were being obtained from individuals and businesses around the district. And, although there cannot have been many, motor vehicles were also being commandeered by the authorities. Reservists working in the Post Office, the police, fire brigade and in various civilian jobs were called up immediately. All cheap and excursion tickets were suspended by the railway and some local residents had been stranded abroad, one family as far away as Switzerland. Miss Robarts of Chislehurst had a difficult journey back from Finland via St Petersburg, Berlin and Belgium. A Penge businessman, on a trip to Leipzig, described his prolonged journey home by train to Flushing and on by boat (probably to Queenborough) which was intercepted in the Medway and fired upon by a patrol boat. His account makes clear what a surprise the outbreak of war had been to him and to his German friends.

The fete and sports day of the Loyal Star of Keston Lodge of Oddfellows planned for 8 August was postponed indefinitely "in consequence of the WAR" and an auction of furniture at Towerfields in Keston was also put off until further notice. However, the "carry on" spirit was not dead "to relieve the tension" a visit to the Grand Hall Electric Theatre at 23 High Street, Bromley, or the Palais de Luxe at 111 High Street, was recommended. At the latter, you could see *The House of Fear* — a thrilling Latin Photo Play and *His Guiding Star*, a striking Pathé

Color Drama. At the Grand Hall there was an Edison Comedy Drama *An American King* which, along with other shows, made it "The Coolest Place of Entertainment in Bromley".

Rather more heated, however, were those newspaper readers who enjoyed the comfort of having a paper brought to their door and who had been experiencing problems. *The Beckenham Journal* asked them not to be impatient over late deliveries and not to:"abuse the boys or telephone in rage to the newsagent".

And so, in a confused but patriotic way, began the transition to war as it impacted on the residents and organisations of the Bromley area.

Sources: *Bromley and District Times* 31July and 7 August 1914
Beckenham Journal/Penge and Sydenham Advertiser 1 and 8 August 1914
Chislehurst and District Times 31 July and 7 August 1914
Kelly's Directories, Wikipedia

The war *was expected to be over by Christmas 1914 but volunteers were still being recruited months later. These Orpington volunteers were pictured at Farnborough in May 1915. The following year conscription was introduced. (BLSL)*

Bromley *was a busy and prosperous market town but the countryside was right on the doorstep. Widmore Road, pictured right, was little more than a country lane.*

Aberdeen Buildings, *below, built in 1889, was typical of the modern parades of shops of that era. It is in the High Street leading to Bromley South station, a highway that was still lined with big houses in 1914. Aberdeen Buildings remains today in the pedestrian area opposite the Churchill Theatre.(MR)*

The Impact of War
Bromley Town 1914 -16

Matthew Greenhalgh

The day after war was declared troops embarked on the train from Bromley South to the accompaniment of patriotic songs and waving of flags. The send-off was officially administered by the Mayor, Mr W Lindley Jones, JP, and his councillors, with the blessing of Rev Canon Tait.

For their families it was the opportunity to raise their men's spirits and support the war effort until they returned for Christmas. It was generally believed the war would be over by then and sons and fathers would be back home. On our island fortress the government urged the maximum centralisation of recruitment, medical aid and funding.

Bromley promptly obliged with a number of courageous men for Kitchener's volunteer force, persuaded by the call to arms echoing — on occasions rather distastefully — from newspaper posters, Bromley Council and other local institutions. By the evening of Friday 13 August, a promising 200 recruits had registered at the Drill Hall in East Street, with more to follow in the following weeks. Each wave of these brave, youthful men was swallowed up by the trenches of Belgium and Northern France. A mass recruitment drive was put into operation. As in other towns, young men in Bromley were treated as outcasts if they refused to enlist. Stories were circulated around the district that: "If your wife and children were being viciously beaten, would you just stand and watch? Of course not! Go off and fight for your country!"

To compensate for hardships brought by enlistment, existing jobs were often kept open for volunteers. Council workmen who joined up retained their full salary less the government's military allowance and soldiers' wives were given free medical treatment. Yet the recruits themselves were given only very basic training, being housed in public buildings commandeered by the Council

" THIS LITTLE PIG STAYED
AT HOME "

before being packed off to war. Their number was joined in February 1915 by specialist motor-drivers, fitters, bakers and butchers who formed the ranks of the expert Army Service Corps.

However, the initial euphoria associated with the first months of the war soon subsided. To counteract this trend, a "Grand Recruitment Rally" was held on Martin's Hill on 2 October 1915, with a march-past of 600 troops from the "West Kents". Such a show of force had its desired effect by swelling the number of Drill Hall volunteers before the year was out.

With the fighters away, the town itself required protection in case of

—BUT SOME PEOPLE WONT GO TILL YOU PUSH 'EM !

Recruiting: there was nothing subtle about the postcards , posters and newspaper adverts urging men to volunteer (MR)

invasion. A home guard was created in the form of the Civilian Training Corps, distinguished by an assortment of armbands.

Essentially, their responsibility was home defence, but they also performed other duties necessary to cope with the strains of war. Men of various ages and backgrounds made up the Corps and could be seen regularly practising their drills on the three council recreation grounds. Alongside this force were the Special Constables, sworn in for duty within one month of the war to support the overburdened local police and ready to deal with the slightest civil disturbance.

Disturbances of both a serious and humorous nature afflicted the town from the commencement of war. One poor man in the first week of fighting was taking his horse to the smithy when he was approached by two artillery men. They stopped him in his tracks, led the horse aside and commandeered it. The British war strategists quite mistakenly believed that the war would be another in a long line of cavalry encounters. Bromley firms lost many of these dependable animals, especially the Tillings omnibus company, the major equine supplier in the district.

Motor vehicles were being requisitioned too. Towards the end of 1914 it was being reported that the Bromley-to-Penge buses had changed route and taken a trip to Belgium! With the additional short supply of petrol, people took to their bikes. The town noted its first-ever bicycle boom — one shop sold 14 on just one Saturday. Another notable occurrence was the patriotic soul who passed through the town with a Union flag on the front of his motor-cycle. However, a darker side to such nationalistic feeling was reflected by the refusal to serve a German-born customer who had reputedly entered Ogden Smith's shop in the High Street and asked for ammunition for his rifle: apparently this could only be purchased by the "right sort of person".

Another problem that became apparent early in the war was that many Bromley residents were stranded abroad, unable to return home. Likewise, foreign-born inhabitants found their lives beset by interruption. Under the Alien Registration policy, all German and Austrian-born citizens were forced to register their names with their local authority. By the end of August 1914, 300

The first casualties *arrived at Bromley South Station on 14 October 1914 and the Red Cross received the instruction to "mobilise all hospitals". Local buildings had been converted into first aid posts for the sick and wounded and nurses were on the platforms with help and refreshments. The cars and vans of well-to-do citizens and local businesses were pressed into service to take the casualties to the Voluntary Aid Detachment hospitals. (BLSL, Joyce Walker collection)*

or so "aliens" had done so in Bromley, and in the following month many were taken to the mass "alien" encampment at Olympia. The South Suburban Gas Company were even more security conscious, placing their works and gasometers off Homesdale Road under permanent guard against spies and saboteurs.

The war effort was to be maintained under all circumstances. At the head of the front line at home were the Voluntary Aid Detachments (See Page 87). Very quickly, relief funds were established to provide them with the necessary resources. When the Red Cross Headquarters received the telephone message at 11pm on 13 October to "mobilise all hospitals" local buildings had already been converted into first aid posts for the sick and wounded.

The cars and vans of well-to-do citizens and local businesses, such as George Pyrke's of the High Street, were pressed into service to ferry the casualties away from the railway station at Bromley South.

Both national and local institutions recognised the need to engender the spirit of action among the people. To provide the necessary finance, labour, transport, manufactured goods, medical aid and supplies for the soldiers fighting across the seas, national initiatives such as the "Ciggy Fund" [to provide cigarettes for the soldiers] were matched in Bromley by ideas like the Mayor's War Fund — to which even children contributed — and Bromley's War Loan Stock offering interest at six and a half per cent.

Although the local community did not run short of money, it was deficient in labour. The public libraries advertised a list of vacancies for voluntary work. Many jobs were snatched up by groups of volunteers such as the Kent Motor Corps or by individuals trained in mechanics and engineering. Women were also quick to come forward. Together with those too old or young to serve, they worked on the district's farms, learnt how to drive essential vans and lorries and eventually joined the London General Omnibus Company as conductors.

At a house in Ravensbourne Road young girls packed parcels for the "heroes" overseas, bearing such gifts as blankets, boot laces, candles, soap, steak puddings and toffees. Parcels were also distributed to prisoners of war, while the wives and daughters of the town were instrumental in the organisation of the special Flag Days for their allies, France (7 July) and Russia (18 November).

Coming together in an energetic drive to sustain the war effort at home had the effect of bringing the local community closer together. Bands played, speeches were made and spirits were lifted. But too often this romanticised picture of "the people's war" has been grossly exaggerated. These patriotic "spirits" had bodies and the bodies needed feeding: soldier and citizen enthusiasm would soon deteriorate on an empty stomach.

National and local operations were devised to sustain the population and the first priority was to find land on which crops could be grown. Since 1878 the amount of agricultural land in Bromley had decreased from 60% to just 31%. The town itself owned little cultivable land, even though plenty of open spaces existed to the south of the borough. Great reliance was thus placed on the economic and efficient farming of allotments, such as those recently established in Tylney Road, and the playing fields or gardens of private individuals and institutions.

To help co-ordinate this "dig for victory", Bromley Rural District Council [the parishes to the south of the borough] appointed a special body which worked closely with the county's War Agricultural Committee. They helped maintain food supplies for the first 18 months of the war, but later problems called for more severe measures such as soup kitchens, control of food prices and customer registration. On the whole, the townspeople co-operated with these and other emergency measures. There was, however, an uglier side to community's reaction. Hoarding of food, for instance, evolved from a social disease into a criminal act, and Bromley had its fair share of criminals. Later, shops were attacked for overcharging on basic foodstuffs. One shopkeeper, German-born Mr FC Ackermann of 13 The Broadway, held his prices beneath the maximum legislated for, yet because of his nationality found his windows smashed by so-called patriots.

With the war, daily life was never the same again. Local leaders encouraged the spirit of "carrying on as usual" in an attempt to play down the dramatic changes. Street improvements continued, people flocked to the religious services on Martin's Hill, Empire Day was celebrated with the usual gusto and the Thursday Market went ahead unabated. Unemployment still remained a problem, now among older men unable to enlist. Yet the lives of the people *did* undergo profound changes. Official reports revealed the increasing incidence of infectious disease and overcrowding. In the field of transport, bus services were either cancelled or curtailed. Throughout the first years of the war, idle gossipers caused panic by spreading stories that the Germans had invaded. The rumours themselves bear witness to the emotive feelings of the time. One particular Bromley gentleman branded all "aliens" spies and showed his emotions by vulgarly abusing his victims in full public view. For his troubles, he was eventually fined 20 shillings [£1] when a Mr Vogel, Austrian-born but British naturalised, took him to court after the 20th such accusation.

Family life was torn apart by fathers and sons marching off to war, many never to return. Mothers now took complete charge of the household. Economies were effected throughout the home, the coal bucket revealed traces of coal slack mixed with clay, newspapers were stacked in the corner, a packet of "Council seeds" lay out the back, and on the stove simmered a meatless stew. School life continued, albeit disrupted, with sons and daughters helping in the school gardens and allotments. Once home, the children collected wild fruit for jam and horse chestnuts for the manufacture of gas mask filters. Even though a measure of distraction for children was eventually provided by activity centres in the town, people were too preoccupied in 1914 and 1915 to give much thought to entertainment. People might enjoy their own amusements — some certainly did, given the 100 illegitimate births that occurred before 1916 — but all the time the impact of war was being felt on a grander scale. By the end of 1915, shops had suffered, businesses had suffered and families had suffered.

On top of this came news of the fighting itself, often distorted but never unmoving.

This is an abridged version of Dr Greenhalgh's article first published in BBLHS's journal Bromleage in February 1994

Government Food Control

*T*he German U-boat campaign against Allied merchant shipping created shortages in raw materials and food. Initially the Government relied on stressing the importance of eating less. Bread, in particular, was a major target when in 1916 the wheat crop failed. It seemed likely there might be insufficient bread for the nation.

A campaign was organised to reduce the amount of bread eaten and to encourage the use of wheat substitutes, and the consumption of bread was reduced to 4lbs per head per week.

By October 1916, coal was in such short supply that it was rationed by the number of rooms a family had in its house.

In July 1917 the government wanted to fix the prices of essential foods, where supply could be controlled. This work was de-centralised to local Food Control Committees who were to enforce the Food Controllers Orders, register the retailers of various foodstuffs and develop food economy campaigns. Local rationing schemes, devised in consultation with the Food Controller, were introduced in late 1917.

In January 1918 sugar became a controlled food and every householder was registered. Butter and margarine were rationed in February, followed by a meat restriction to 15oz per person per week and bacon to 5oz per head. In July 1918 tea was rationed to 2oz per person.

Some of the shortages were offset by an increase in gardening activity. From the beginning of the war there was an emphasis on self-sufficiency and the Ministry of Agriculture produced leaflets on topics such as pig and rabbit breeding, feeding of poultry and the cultivation of onions and fruit.

Allotments had been in existence since the previous century but as food became scare Parish Councils and some landowners made more land available for cultivation. In 1917, the government took over 2.5 million acres of land for farming. By the end of the war, Britain had an extra three million acres of farming land.

Bromley's Thursday Market,
pictured below, was held throughout
the war in the market square. The
Food Control Office operated from the
town hall in the centre of the square.
The manager, Mr Brooks, is pictured
right with, centre, Nellie Jessop.
The town hall was built in the 1860s
and originally the basement was used
for the market while there were offices
and the Literary Institute reading room
above. By the outbreak of war a new
library had been built, now replaced
by the Churchill Theatre and Bromley
Library, and the market was held
outside. The 19th-century town hall
was demolished to make way for the
current buildings in 1932.
(MR and BLSL)

TOWN-HALL · MARKET-SQUARE
1st World War   BROMLEY
Kent

Market Day.   Bromley.

The Wrench Series, No. 4606

35

The Derby Scheme
Recruitment in Beckenham 1915

Cliff Watkins

The generally-held belief in 1914 was that the war would be "over by Christmas". But Christmas passed and by the summer of 1915 there had been a decline in voluntary recruitment despite raising the upper age limit to 38.

Many in government were reluctant to bring in compulsory military service, so in July they passed the National Registration Act — which became known as the Derby Scheme after the Secretary of State for War, Edward Stanley, the 17th Earl of Derby.

The idea was that men who voluntarily registered their name would be called upon for service only when necessary. Married men had an added incentive in that they were advised they would be called up only once the supply of single men was exhausted. The scheme was also referred to as the "Group System" as men were classified in groups according to their year of birth and marital status and were to be called up with their group when it was required.

At a national level, the scheme proved unsuccessful and was abandoned in December 1915, in spite of the fact that the execution of Nurse Edith Cavell by the Germans on 12 October 1915 was used in recruitment rallies. It was superseded by the Military Service Act 1916, which introduced conscription.

A total of 215,000 men enlisted while the scheme was operational, and another 2,185,000 attested for later enlistment. However, 38% of single men and 54% of married men who were not in "starred" [protected, high or scarce skill] occupations failed to come forward.

In Beckenham and Penge men did come forward, as detailed in the town's broadsheet newspaper, the *Beckenham Journal*, edited and published by Tom Thornton, the founder of modern Beckenham. He was a keen supporter of the scheme and a man who knew how to persuade his readers to rally behind a cause. In 1913 he had galvanised the town's population in a successful attempt to secure most of the Kelsey Manor estate as a park for the townspeople.

As WWI unfolded, he declared: "The *Journal's* coverage of the war is about men on service who have been wounded/killed/promoted/merited. All the *Beckenham Journal* is interested in is that, when the war is over, the roll we have been trying to keep since the outbreak will remain an historical record for the use of generations to come."

In the five issues from 4 December 1915 to 1 January 1916, the *Journal* disclosed the names and addresses of more than 1,700 local men who had registered for the Derby Scheme, and devoted a whole page of the Christmas issue to recognising their patriotism.

BJ Issue date	Beckenham	Penge*	Others**	Total
1915, Dec 4	36	44	57	137
1915, Dec 11	80	89	13	182
1915, Dec 18	135	75	9	219
1915, Dec 25	323	286	60	669
1916, Jan 1	182	333	16	531
Total	756	827	155	1738

* *including Anerley*
** *West Wickham, Shortlands, Hayes, Keston, Downe & Cudham,*

The figure of 756 recruits in one month from Beckenham is chilling. The roll call of those who died during the 51 months of the war, and are remembered on the Beckenham War Memorial, is 711.

They include two of Tom Thornton's sons, Hedley and Stanley. Both were in service before the Derby Scheme. Hedley died of influenza in January 1916 and Stanley was killed in action in May 1917.

The difficulties of farming
and the impact of the war on everyday life were recorded by George James "JG" Miller, top left, in his letters to his serving sons Stanley, above, and "Jumbo" left. Both boys survived the war but it was their younger brothers who carried on farming at Court Lodge. (SM)

My Dear Stanley

Letters from a Chelsfield farmer

Patrick Hellicar

A remarkable record of the impact of the Great War on Bromley's agricultural community has been preserved in letters written by Chelsfield farmer George James Miller — known as "GJ" — to his two eldest sons who had volunteered to "do their bit". Although covering only eight months, from September 1915 to May 1916, they reveal the changes and challenges facing folk back home, as well as a father's deep anxiety for his boys.

Every week, mostly on Sunday evenings, George Miller sat down to write his letters in his study-cum-office at Court Lodge Farm. Scrawling in a stream-of-consciousness style in two books of headed notepaper that he also used for business correspondence, GJ took a carbon copy of everything. Thus, his thoughts and feelings were captured for posterity.

Often, he felt tired and unwell, suffering from stress and neuritis. At first he had only to pen a few lines to his eldest son, George Harold Stanley (known as Stanley), who was stationed in Malta with the Motor Transport division of the Army Service Corps and celebrated his 21st birthday on 24 September 1915, one day after his father's 45th. Soon, however, GJ was also writing to his second son, Cecil Aubrey Alexander, called "Jumbo" by the family, who enlisted in the Royal Naval Air Service 12 days before Christmas that year at the age of 18.

"My Dear Stanley", GJ usually began, or sometimes "My Dear Stan". It was the same for No. 2 son: "My Dear Cecil" or "My Dear Jum". He always signed off with "Best love from us all. Your affectionate Father". Along with his letters he sent each boy a copy of the *Orpington District Times* and a £1 or 10 shilling note to enable them to buy a few extra comforts.

With more than 700 acres on his hands — Court Lodge Farm at

Chelsfield, neighbouring land acquired from the Goddington estate plus Fairtrough Farm 2½ miles away at Pratts Bottom — and with wide social and business contacts as well as family farming at Crockenhill, Sanderstead and Mitcham, GJ was in a good position to observe events, form strong opinions and make down-to-earth comments.

His first letter in the 1915 book addressed to Stanley is dated 20 September, though it is clear Stan had been away for a while [he enlisted in October 1914], that they corresponded regularly and that Stan's mother, Emily, wrote separately. Like her husband, Emily was often under the weather — hardly surprising, as only a few months before, at the age of 43, she had given birth to her seventh child.

GJ kept his absent sons up to date on how family, friends, neighbours and business acquaintances were faring. He also passed on snippets about local men who were about to enlist or had gone off to war already, and any news of casualties among them. As farmers do, he focused on the weather, labour problems, rising costs and market matters. But he touched on national political and economic affairs too.

On 29 September he informed Stanley that trade at Borough Market [Southwark] was good. But, in his first references to the impact of army recruitment draining men from farm work, he was cautious about the outlook, saying: "We are putting every bit of land possible down to corn as the labour question is so bad."

Such difficulties meant a great number of people were giving up their farms, GJ noted, adding: "There are any amount of farm sales this Michaelmas." The Budget and higher taxes (delivered on 21 September by the new Chancellor, Reginald McKenna) looked like hitting everyone very hard, he asserted.

Four days later GJ reported that he had been to three farm sales in a week. At Rainham, in Essex, 33 horses were auctioned — "10 of them fetched a good bit over 100 guineas, the best one fetching 145 guineas ... more than they were worth at the present time". At Addington Lodge (Croydon), he "bought several things, including two horses, one at 77 gns and the other at 70 gns", which he thought cheap. At that time thousands of horses were being snapped up by the army every month for use in the supply lines and on the battlefields.

Meanwhile, the "labour question" was troubling: "It seems the more they earn, the worse they are, but I am in hopes that when the hopping finishes we shall get on a bit better."

By 11 October a new factor had emerged. "The labour question gets worse every week, especially now they are building the [Canadian army] hospital at The Boundaries [in Orpington]," he told Stanley. "They are paying ordinary labourers 6d [2½p] an hour working all day Saturday and Sunday as it <u>has</u> to be finished in 11 weeks." No wonder GJ was unhappy: the minimum wage for agricultural labourers was 3½d an hour in 1914.

Trade generally was still good, his letter noted, with onions going for £10 to £11 per ton, having risen from £8 in a couple of weeks. Eventually, they reached £16. Potatoes were good too, but "as we are so short-handed we are clamping them up [putting them in temporary storage under straw and soil]". By the end of April, they hit £11 a ton.

GJ told of a Saturday evening trip to London with Emily "to have some dinner and to see the London darkness", which he described as "absolutely fearful as you really cannot see where you are". Apart from lighting restrictions and blackouts, the reality of war was coming home in other ways. "It is most depressing over here now, as almost everyone you speak to has someone related to them either wounded or killed and what to think of things I really don't know, or when it will be the end of it all," he said.

Out of the blue, a postcard arrived from the wife of Stanley's Colonel instructing the Millers that mail for the battalion should now be addressed to "Mediterranean Expedition". They feared their son had been sent to Egypt or the Dardanelles but on 20 October a letter from Stan brought a mixture of relief and concern. Next day, GJ wrote to him: "So thankful to think you were still at Malta, although I must say it worries me very much to hear that you were not considered by the doctor fit for active service as I cannot understand what it means ... Anyhow, whatever it is, you cannot be any worse off than you would have been to have gone with the others under the present conditions, which I think are awful."

F. Julyan, Photo　　　　CHELSFIELD.

Chelsfield village has hardly changed in 100 years. It is a conservation area and there has been very little new building. The only differences today from these early 20th century views of the village centre are that the shops are now houses and cars line the street. Above, the Five Bells and Cross Hall and, below, the shops opposite the Five Bells. However, in 1928, Court Road, the Orpington bypass (A224) — known at the time as New Road — divided the village from its church, St Martin of Tours, and also cut through the Millers' farm. (OHO Jean Bodfish collection)

Chelsfield, Kent.

Bringing Stanley up to date on home news, he said: "What a time we are having over here with Zep [Zeppelin] raids &c. I really don't know what things are coming to. Fortunately they have not reached our district yet."

He went on: "The labour question is still very bad and looks like getting worse now that they <u>really</u> mean getting so many soldiers. I hear some of the neighbours are paying women 3s-6d a day and carting them to and from [St Mary] Cray."

Over the next few weeks, GJ was much exercised by the climate. In fact, it heralded a period of extraordinary weather that lasted almost to the following April and included torrential rain, strong winds, hail, bitter cold, sharp frosts, deep snow and blizzard-like conditions. January, on the other hand, turned out to be the mildest for more than 50 years.

By 24 October 1915 the weather had changed from "delightful for the time of the year" to very rainy and cold. At the beginning of November GJ told how London had been cloaked in dense fog for two days: "You cannot imagine what London looks like with its present [restricted] lighting and thick fog. About the only bright spot was around our lamp [presumably at the Millers' market stand] which, being under the arch, we are allowed to use."

Amid all this, trade was "fairly good" but shortage of labour was making life difficult. A lot of young greengrocers were expecting to have to shut up their shops and join the armed forces, GJ said. Market porters were doing well, though: "They get ½d per bag for carrying our cabbage and as much as 3d and 4d a turn for box stuff."

Work patterns had had to change. "I am starting sending the engine up in the daytime with the stuff instead of at night as it is not safe to go out at night now that the lighting is so bad," GJ said. "You have no idea how trying it is to try to do business under the present conditions as no one cares whether they work or not."

A week later he grumbled to Stan: "Everything here is absolutely rotten and I am just about fed up with it all but I suppose one must stick it."

On 16 November a heavy snowstorm added to his woes. "We had the greatest difficulty in getting through it to Bromley," GJ

Farmers had to be inventive and forward thinking during the First World War when labourers and horses were in short supply. This speeded up the transition to motorised transport on the farm. Above, ploughing on Court Lodge farm (SM) and, below, a Miller truck from the early 1920s. (AC)

reported. "I think it was the worst journey I ever remember." On the 21st he wrote: "It took the engine seven hours to get two vans from Foxbury to the main road on Friday [a distance of only a mile or so]."

GJ also told of another local change spurred by the war. "Vickers of Erith are running buses to and from Orpington for munition workers and they are taking all the available houses to house them," he said. Ever the businessman, he let Harecroft, a property in Warren Road, Chelsfield, to Vickers for £50 a year.

With manpower problems on the farm increasing, GJ travelled to Bromley to see a Martin Motor Plough in action. "It does its work well, it makes two furrows at a time and only needs one man and will do about four acres a day," he noted. "It only costs £185 nett and looks like being a valuable tool now that horses are so dear."

So impressed was he that the following month, after three visits in one week to the Smithfield Show, GJ bought an American-made Overtime ploughing tractor. He got a potato planter "on appro" [approval] as well. "If it works properly, it will plant 7-8 acres a day with one horse and man," he told Stanley on 12 December.

The machines were not delivered until February, however, and he had to fit extensions to widen the tractor wheels to 18 inches to stop it sinking in the mud. Despite numerous problems, he described it as working "wonderfully well", though he sacked the "old fool", Hills, who drove it into a tree, breaking the axle. In his place, he took on a 25 year-old rejected by the army.

Also occupying GJ was the Derby Scheme (See P36) which demanded a personal canvass of every man between the ages of 18 and 41. Each was asked either to join up voluntarily at once or attest and be called upon later to serve.

At first GJ refused to carry out the task among his workers and returned the papers, but quickly came under pressure. "There was quite a to-do about my refusing to canvass our men, the Conservative Agent coming over from Bromley to try and get me to do it," he confided to Stanley on 29 November. "So after all I agreed, although all of them being married I was not very

45

successful. The most I could get out of them was that they would join when all the single men had done so." Only George Whitehead said he would sign up "but, of course, he was rejected".

Stanley's brother Jumbo (Cecil), afraid he might be "pushed in some rotten infantry lot" if he waited until forced to join up, tried to get into the Royal Naval Air Service but there were no vacancies. Unexpectedly, though, he was accepted, subject to a medical, by the RNAS on 11 December. On the 19th GJ described to Stanley how Jumbo, instead of being sent to Sheerness along with most of the new recruits, was picked out and packed off with 13 others to Felixstowe in Suffolk, where the RNAS station had "some wonderful seaplanes".

Despite anxieties now for two sons, GJ asserted: "I would much rather have it like that than to be like dear old Bowen, the timber merchant [at Halstead]. Neither of his noble sons have joined, he says he could not spare them. I think neither he nor they would be missed much for all the good they are to the country but I suppose they are like a lot more of the shirkers who are willing to skulk at home while the men go and do their bit."

In the market, a new problem surfaced. He told Jumbo on 21 December the Millers had been "a lot of stuff short" and found they were "losing it off the stand in the night". He solved the problem by posting a night watchman and taking on an extra porter so goods could be moved out more quickly.

Early in the New Year, fields at Fairtrough were being prepared, the steam plough making "a fine job of it". But very mild and wet weather prevented the farmer "getting the best out of what little labour we have left". Trade was better "but nothing great". However, GJ had been holding back his wheat stocks from sale and was pleased to think it was "going to get very dear".

He was also more cheerful about the war. "I somehow think it will not last beyond next Autumn," he wrote on 4 January.

But by the 25th, GJ was "beastly tired". Trade was very bad, he told Stanley, adding: "It absolutely gives me the hump to go to market at all." Fortunately, "several fresh men" had come to help on the farm and he had found a "very decent man" to drive the still-awaited new tractor plough.

That day, he noted, soldiers of the 7th City of London Battalion stationed at the former Fox's Brewery at Green Street Green had left for Aldershot and 1,400 HAC [Hon Artillery Company] men had taken their place. A few weeks later, he opined sniffily: "The men at the Green, although some are of course very good class chaps, the others seem very ordinary."

At the end of January, GJ reported: "The labour question is the most serious question we have to contend with as we have to pay such high prices for piecework. Our wages this week came to over £80 but some people would say we are lucky to have to pay it as in some parts they can hardly get a man at all. But with stuff fetching such awful prices it gives me a bit of an anxious time."

Now he was hoping to employ an assistant. "I think if I could get a man who understands farming a bit and who is well up in clerical work it would be a great help to me," he wrote. He wanted someone to handle his selling in the market and all his office work to allow him to keep a closer eye on the farm. This was partly due to the fact that he was now required to keep separate accounts for the farm and for his other business of hiring out his "steam tackle" [machinery] to plough other farmers' fields at 18 shillings an acre. "It's a bit more profitable than vegetable farming just now," he explained to Jumbo.

It was hard to find a suitable assistant, though. A 46-year-old man was given a trial but he was "not smart enough". Another candidate dropped out. In late February, GJ related: "He did not come as his missus said the market work would kill him in a very little while. I was very sorry as he seemed a very jolly chap. He was 39, a public school chap ineligible for the Army on account of his health. He had had an Auctioneer & Valuer business but got crippled through the war. He said he lost over £1000 in 18 months."

Fortunately, by the end of March he had taken on an "excellent salesman" who had worked in Covent Garden for more than 20 years. Over the following months, he proved to be all GJ hoped for.

Also on GJ's mind were cars. Tax on them had increased and petrol prices had rocketed from 1s-10d [9p] a gallon at the start of the war to 2s-10d [14p] by 1916. "Fed up" with the family's Talbot, and their Peugeot suffering starting troubles and worn bearings, impossible to get tyres for and "not strong enough for this hilly district", he reckoned he could manage with one car if he took up horse-riding again — which he did, and at the end of April wrote: "It seems to suit me well."

He tried out a three-year-old 25-horsepower Fiat on sale at Smith & Milroy in Orpington for about £200, then a 15hp Stoewer of the same age. "I think I might make them an offer for it," he told Jumbo on 30 January. Perhaps suddenly mindful of its German origins, GJ steered clear of the Stoewer and in April bought a year-old American-made Overland with 4,000 miles on the clock instead. "It is a delightful car to drive," he enthused in a letter to Stanley. "When it gets warm you have to put your ear to the bonnet to tell whether the engine is running or not."

In February the household found its domestic staff reduced to one maid and a nurse. "Servants are almost unobtainable now that there is so much work for women in munition works,

The farmhouse of Court Lodge Farm *where the Miller family still live today. The farm and the machinery business started by GJ after the First World War are still run by his great-grandson Steve Miller. (CH)*

48

motor bus driving, conducting etc," GJ complained to Stanley. "You would not know the place over here now."

A month later, he was worrying again about farm labour as attested married men were about to be called up. "They say we must use women but of course there is not much that they can do," he wrote to Stanley. And to Jumbo: "You say you think we might be able to get some of our married men put back [given temporary exemption]. I am very doubtful about it as the local tribunal are granting very few exemptions now ... I suppose we must try to get along with women."

Efforts being made by local farmers, market people and others to avoid the call-up were a recurring theme in GJ's letters over the months. On 20 March he told Stanley: "It makes my blood boil to see the scheming that is going on to get young fellows exempted when men are wanted so badly, especially when your own have gone 'like the old-fashioned Britisher' of their own free will."

Word of his views and farming expertise appears to have spread. At the end of the month Sir Mark Collet, a Kemsing landowner who chaired the military Appeal Tribunal in Bromley, asked GJ to advise on the merits of various appeals for exemption.

Having done so, GJ told his sons on 16 April: "Now they want me to represent the Board of Ag [Agriculture] at the local Tribunals. I told them I don't want the job, but will do it if absolutely necessary. I expect I shall have to as they must have someone that understands the local agricultural conditions ... From what I can see of things they will want a lot more men yet, but they are beginning to realise that there is a limit to the number they may take from the land." He took on the role, however, and pursued it diligently despite all the other calls on his time and energy.

In one of his last letters in the 1916 book, GJ mused: "How the time drags on. It seems ages since you were here. How I do wish it were all over and you were both able to come back." The brothers did, in fact, survive the war. Stanley lived until the age of 76, dying in 1971, while Jumbo passed away at 86 in 1983.

Ironically, their Affectionate Father, GJ, was killed in the Second World War when his car collided head-on with an army truck on Court Road, Chelsfield, in 1943. He was 72 years-old.

A small village, West Wickham had a population of
around 1,300 souls in 1914 and large houses,
including the grand Ravenswood mansion, lined the
High Street. This view of the High Street is looking from
The Swan public house towards Croydon. The cottage
on the far right was the post office 100 years ago and
today is a hairdressers and barbers. The buildings in
the distance on the left are now Lloyds and Barclays
banks. (PL)

A Village at War

West Wickham

Joyce Walker

In 1911 the population of West Wickham was 1302; in 1921, 1301. The intervening years had seen the Great War and with it the grievous loss of 78 men and many others mutilated and disabled.

When war was declared the Lennard family was well to the fore. Sir Henry Lennard was Lord of the Manor and a Lieutenant-Colonel in the Kent Artillery Militia. Together with a Captain Reid, he had already been busy scouting the countryside for horses for use by the army. Lady Lennard, already president of the local Red Cross, was made president of the local branch of the Soldiers' and Sailors' Families Association and Miss Grace Lennard was in training as a member of the Voluntary Aid Detachment (VAD).

During the year, members of the local Red Cross had arranged for the loan of various houses for use as auxiliary hospitals in case of emergency: Wood Lodge, The Warren, Coney Hall, Hayes Grove. All these arrangements were brought to a state of readiness. The Boy Scouts were soon in action, undertaking patrol duties on the railway line between Lewisham and Dartford, in conjunction with the 14th Greenwich Troop.

Farmers were concerned with retaining their employees for, by the end of the war, despite exemptions, some 300 men had enlisted in the colours, and eventually it became necessary to use members of the Women's Land Army. At times, convalescent patients from the nearby military hospital at Addington helped out with the light work.

As part of the response to Lord Kitchener's appeal for 100,000 men, a meeting was held in the Lecture Hall on 22 August 1914. There must have been a good result from that meeting, for on 5 September it was announced that the football club was unable to field a team, "the young men of the village making such a good response to the country's call to arms".

Another call to arms came at 11 o'clock on the evening of 13 October, when the Red Cross Detachment, as other detachments of the Red Cross in Kent, was ordered to set up its hospitals ready for an influx of wounded soldiers. One can only imagine the impact a military hospital had on the village — up to this time, wars were happening overseas, now their casualties were on its very doorstep.

The *Beckenham Journal* reported that "practically every day some of the wounded soldiers are taken out for motor drives and others may be seen walking about on the common. They appear a very cheerful set of fellows and on one occasion, borrowed a pick-axe from a man working on the road and for quite a long time enjoyed themselves in helping the roadman in his work".

Tranquil West Wickham High Street *seen from outside the Wheatsheaf public house looking up the High Street. Several of the cottages have survived but have been converted into shops. (PL)*

The first casualty of the war with a West Wickham connection was Lance Corporal HJ Kemp of the 16th Lancers, who was killed on the first day of the Battle of Mons on 23 August 1914, soon to be followed by Private T Smith and Private E Butcher, both from the Royal West Surrey Regiment.

War was, indeed, now a reality. Against this background of grief and worry, life went on much as usual. Some activities and entertainments were curtailed, but others sprang up in their place. Proceeds of concerts in the Lecture Hall were now devoted, in the main, to war charities. Patriotic entertainments were given by the Allies from Beckenham, in aid of the Prince of Wales Fund for National Relief; the Pom-poms from West Wickham sang for the Kentish Prisoners of War, and Frank Stoner organised concerts in aid of the Red Cross and the Belgian refugees.

The Rector organised services of intercession for the war, illustrated by lantern pictures and he also showed pictures of the war and spoke on "Causes and Commencement of the war" and "Serbia and the Serbians".

Not all news was of the war. At the end of 1914, a terrible gale and blizzard swept the area. The *Beckenham Journal* reported: "In many of the fields, several trees which must have reached a ripe old age were uprooted and in other cases, large branches were torn away from the trees by the wind. The falling of two giant elms at the cross-roads at the bottom of Corkscrew Hill was undoubtedly the cause of a great deal of anxiety in the village. The roots of one burst a gas main and almost immediately the effects of the burst were felt in a number of houses in the village. About 9 o'clock all gas lights began to dim and gradually they went out altogether. There was a run on oil-lamps and candles. The street lamps which were but few and far between also went. West Wickham was for two or three nights in complete darkness."

This blackout was a foretaste of things to come. In May 1916 the parish council decided, in the interests of economy, that there should be no more street lighting until the war ended.

Trees were not all that fell. In April 1915, on Easter Monday, an Admiralty air balloon came down in a field near the railway

Into uniform *The 16 young men above were pictured in the garden of The Swan, shortly after becoming the first West Wickham volunteers.(BLSL, Joyce Walker collection) Below, army manoeuvres on West Wickham Hill. (PL)*

station, no doubt exciting the hundreds of people spending the day in West Wickham Woods and on Hayes Common.

Nineteen fifteen saw the start of two new ventures: one of a practical nature and the other with a high moral tone. First, Mrs Henfrey under the auspices of the Red Cross, formed the Langley Park Working Party, whose members made articles for the troops - pyjamas, underwear, socks, bedsocks, operation stockings, mufflers, bed-jackets, kettle holders, roller bandages, comfort bags and the like. Regular participants received a badge marked VW, but were obliged to pay a penny a session for lighting and cottons.

Second, Lady Lennard organised a League of Honour "[which] aims at helping women in their efforts to build up a purer and better England, so that our country may be more worthy of the sacrifices that are being made for her".

Those sacrifices were mounting: in the early months of 1915, eight more names were added to the list of dead.

But the most devastating incident of the war to affect West Wickham came in the shape of the battle of Loos on 25 September 1915. For West Wickham it was a tragedy — eight men were killed, (six in three days), four were wounded and one made a prisoner of war. During September and October, six more names found their way on to the list of those killed in action. In all, 22 men lost their lives in 1915, the highest figure of all the war years.

It was not at all surprising to find that the local paper reported a dearth of young men — "it being a pleasing reflection on the village life that almost every man physically capable of bearing arms has joined some branch or other of HM Forces". Many families had more than one member in the Forces: there were six Uzzells, five Kibbles, five Hardys, four Russells, four Percivals, four Millingtons and there were several more with three representatives.

Early 1916 saw ventures at home to raise funds for the Kentish prisoners of war, beginning in January with a flag day, which raised the sum of £6-12-11½d. [£6.65p] The Misses Moule organised concerts in the Lecture Hall in February and March.

The West Kent Tribunal sat for the first time at Bromley Court House and rejected Harold Robson's appeal for exemption as a stockman. Ernest Weller, a chauffeur with a widowed mother to support, had his appeal for exemption rejected and his was the doubtful distinction, as a private in the Sussex Regiment, to be the last Wickham man to die in action on 4 November 1918.

It was a difficult time for farmers. Thomas Marden Jnr, in charge of several farms, was granted six weeks' exemption in June; William Dean, one of only two cowmen on Coney Hall Farm, was granted a conditional exemption; Cecil Miller, cowman and market gardener for Mr Justin, lost his appeal and was passed for general service. Other troubles: in May, William Andrew and Charles Stockbridge were each fined 40 shillings [£2] for infringing the Lighting Order.

The year 1916 added 19 more names to the roll of honour, now numbering 44. The local papers carried many anguished appeals for news of those posted missing. Home life, even without the constant grief and worry, was becoming increasingly difficult. Under the Defence of the Realm Act (DORA), controls were placed on many aspects of life. In January 1917, Frank Reed was fined 10 shillings [50p] for keeping 20 homing pigeons at the Home Farm without a permit. No doubt the Temperance Society rejoiced in the fact that public houses were open only in the evenings, "treating" forbidden and beer reduced in strength and made more expensive.

In March a new Order came into effect and bread could not be sold unless it was 12 hours old and had to be in the shape of a one-piece oven-bottom loaf, or a tin loaf, or a roll: no currant, sultana or milk bread could be sold or sugar used in the making of bread. Even the older girls at the National School were given a cookery demonstration on bread substitutes. Fortunately, living in the country, most people grew their own vegetables and with the provision of allotments, it could have been very much worse.

The civilian population would have observed and breathed sighs of relief when the Zeppelins passed overhead on their way to and from London, and heard the crash of bombs on Croydon and Beckenham. One bomb fell in a field in Coney Hall, close enough to Wickham Court for the butler to believe that it had fallen on his garden cottage, but in fact it was about half a mile away.

Kent Lane at 1.45am on a stormy night in August was the

setting for some excitement when two German escaped prisoners of war from Holyport Camp at Maidenhead were discovered in a hedge by "a smart mongrel with collie and foxhound blood". They were arrested by PC Cleever, who was cycling near the waterworks with the said dog. PC Cleever said that he was helped by a knowledge of Yiddish picked up while serving in London.

By November 1917 three members of the Gayler family had been killed. The number of dead had now risen to 62 and there

How DORA restricted the realm

In 1917, Frank Reed was fined 10 shillings under the Defence of the Realm Act (DORA) for keeping pigeons at Home Farm, West Wickham, without a permit.

The Act controlled a great many freedoms people had taken for granted before the war. Movement was restricted in some areas, such as military establishments, and visitors needed permit books, pictured right, to gain entry.

The Act enabled the government to seize property, apply censorship guidelines, make regulations regarding criminal offences, and control labour as deemed necessary for the duration of the war. More regulations came in as the war progressed.

Forbidden to the public

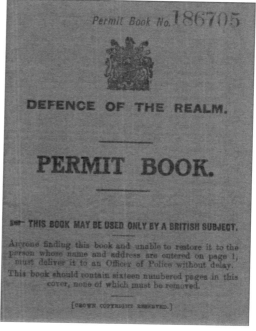

Permit Book No. 186705

DEFENCE OF THE REALM.

PERMIT BOOK.

THIS BOOK MAY BE USED ONLY BY A BRITISH SUBJECT.

Anyone finding this book and unable to restore it to the person whose name and address are entered on page 1, must deliver it to an Officer of Police without delay.

This book should contain sixteen numbered pages in this cover, none of which must be removed.

[CROWN COPYRIGHT RESERVED.]

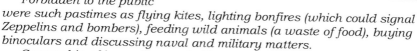

were such pastimes as flying kites, lighting bonfires (which could signal Zeppelins and bombers), feeding wild animals (a waste of food), buying binoculars and discussing naval and military matters.

Censorship of journalism and of letters coming home from the front line was imposed. People who breached the regulations with intent to assist the enemy could be sentenced to death. Ten such executions took place.

was much sorrow in West Wickham. Gone was the idealism of the early years, to be replaced by the bitterness engendered by the loss of so many young men.

By now there was a feeling in the village that the dead should be honoured in some way and the September 1917 issue of the parish magazine invited suggestions for some kind of war shrine.

Parcels were sent to those soldiers and sailors who had managed to evade the casualty lists. Interestingly enough, the contents differed between the Services. The soldiers got steak pudding, mince pie, dates, tin soup cubes, potted meat, toffee, candles, soap, buttons, boot-laces. The sailors were sent steak pudding, mince pie, fruit cake, dates, potted meat, toffee, peppermint.

In 1918 food rationing was introduced, with sugar being rationed from January. In April, ration cards were issued for meat, bacon, butter, cheese and margarine and only tea, cheese and bread remained unrestricted. A communal kitchen was set up in the village and power was given to the organising committee to purchase a consignment of pickled herrings. The entire village was now committed to supporting the war effort. The Bible Class made a collection and sent 7s-6d [37½p] to each soldier and sailor on active service and five shillings [25p] to each hospital patient. Thirty pairs of socks were knitted by the children and a special War Savings effort was made by them with the purchase of six "Feed the Guns" certificates.

By 1917, Mrs Henfrey and her friends in the Working Party, had sent no fewer than 480 items to the Red Cross Headquarters. As the war moved into its fourth year, several urgent appeals were received, as a result of which, the following articles were made and despatched: 102 pairs pyjamas, 24 pairs pants, two pairs

> **To combat food loss through rat and sparrow activities, West Wickham Parish Council provided rat traps for the older children, who were paid a halfpenny for each tail and one penny for each sparrow's head.**

operation stockings, 12 helpless case shirts, 90 roller bandages, 27 hotwater bottle covers, 50 limb pillows. 30 vests, 67 pairs day socks, 13 mufflers, 14 bed-jackets, 20 kettle holders, 263 comfort bags.

The Working Party boasted a junior section organised by Miss McAndrew and Miss Lennard. The children worked mainly during the school holidays. They too, made bed-jackets, hot-water bottle covers, kettle holders and limb pillows. Personal parcels were sent to the 11 prisoners-of-war — among their contents were: pipe, sponge, pencils, tooth powder, pomade, cap badge, badges of rank, stick of shaving soap, shaving-brush, razor, mohair bootlaces, health salts, insecticide powder, combs, hair and toothbrushes, buttons, braces and belt, chess, draughts, dominoes, dubbin, hobnails, 8oz sweets, medal ribbons, brass polish, mittens and a muffler.

At 11 o'clock on the 11th day of the 11th month of the year 1918, the maroons used as air-raid warnings boomed for the last time. The war was over, but at what cost? In West Wickham it amounted to 78 dead, at least 41 wounded, 10 ill and 11 prisoners of war, one of whom was repatriated. The tally of decorations was impressive and included two DSOs, four DCMs, five MCs, five MMs, one DSM, four Mentioned in Despatches, one Croix de Guerre (Belgium), and one St George's Russian Medal (2nd Class).

Sources

Beckenham Journal and Bromley Mercury
Personal recollections by Mrs G Thompson and Mrs L Robjant
St John's Parish Magazine
Battle of Loos by Philip Warne
Census Returns, Street Directories, National School Log Book
Red Cross Archives
Greystones 1911-1963
West Wickham Parish Council Minutes
The Times History of the War

This is an abridged version of the article written by the late Joyce Walker and first published in 1982 in Bromley Local History No.6
The Joyce Walker archive is now held in Bromley Local Studies Library

The part of Bromley Common *where the Newby family settled was the area bounded by Bromley Common, Homesdale Road and Crown Lane. It was centred on the thriving shopping centre in Chatterton Road, which had been developed from the later years of the 19th century. The drawing above shows Crown Lane in 1905, looking towards Southborough Lane. The Newbys lived in a "modern" development off Salisbury Lane to the left. St Luke's Church, Bromley Common, below, opened in 1887, but was not fully completed until 1910.(BLSL)*

Through the Eyes of a Child
Bromley Common

Nancy Tubb

The Newby family of Nancy, sister Nora, their parents and Syd,
a young lad who lived with them, moved to 22 Balfour Road,
Bromley Common, in 1913 when Mr Newby, who worked on
the railway, became a signalman at Bickley Station. Later in life
Nancy Tubb recalled her wartime childhood and her
years at Addison Road School.

I remember sitting in school and seeing pictures on the wall of Edith Cavell,[1] who was a nurse in Belgium. She was shot by the Germans, accused of being a spy. Then there was a picture of Lord Kitchener pointing a finger at you, saying: "Your Country Needs You".

The teachers always seemed to be dressed in black and crying and the big girls used to whisper to us that they had "lost someone during the war". As we walked along Chatterton Road we would see quite young ladies dressed in black with black veils attached to the back of their hats. I told my mother I would like to wear one when I grew up. She informed me that they were called widows' weeds and they wore them because their husbands had been killed in the war.

I remember the night that Silvertown[2] was bombed and we looked out of our bedroom window and saw the sky all aglow and my mother saying: "All those poor people." The thing I didn't like when I lay in bed at night during the war was the searchlight. We had Venetian blinds and these lights used to shine all round the room if there was an air raid.

There was excitement when one of our guns shot down an airship at Cuffley in Essex [in fact Hertfordshire].[3] That was at the beginning of the war. Later the aeroplanes came. One night, during an air raid over London, a German plane was shot down and fell on a house at Valley Road, Shortlands, killing everyone living there. As it was on the outskirts of Bromley, close to Martin's Hill my mother and father took us all to see the damage. I thought it was dreadful. (How we used to walk in those days! I could have been only about five and a half.) Later another plane came down in the Whitehall Recreation Ground and into some of the back gardens of Southlands Road, but no-one was hurt, only windows broken.

Another day I had taken Syd and my sister in her pushchair, into the rec to play and I remember thinking: "We are the only ones here!" And then my mother appeared, dressed only in her indoor clothes, saying: "Why didn't you come home when the warden sounded the warning?" I couldn't have heard it.

I remember at night that the Duddys [who lived] next door to us and Mrs Duddy's mother and sister all used to come into our house with all their children. Mother used to push the kitchen table into the alcove under the stairs and we children used to sit there. All the grown-ups sat in a half-circle round the kitchen range with a small case or a bag beside them. I suppose it must have held all their valuables.

My father didn't have to go to war because he failed the medical. He had had rheumatic fever when he was young. But he did join the Chislehurst Volunteers. We used to go and watch him sometimes doing his drill on Chislehurst Common. Then a bomb fell on the common one day, so of course we all had to go and see the crater.[4] Not a bit like the last war.

Mr Maynard [a neighbour] was in the Light Infantry and had to look after the horses. They used horses a lot at the beginning of the war until the mechanical tanks had come into use. Mr Duddy was in the Flying Corps so we kids thought he was very grand in his grey/blue uniform. We thought he was really wonderful flying those aeroplanes but afterwards learned he was in the stores department.

My father had to work 12-hour shifts at the [Bickley] signal box. Syd and I used to take his dinner to him after mother had cooked it. We carried it in a little basket, called him when we got to the fence on the bridge that crossed the road, and he would come and collect it. It was a very great treat if he took us into the signal box but we got an even greater thrill if there was an engine on the turntable.

At Orpington there was a hospital for wounded Canadian soldiers very close to the railway station. As my father was a St John's Ambulance man he might have to go at any time of the night or day to unload the wounded soldiers.[5] The trains were white with red crosses on them and used to be shunted on to the line that was beside the hospital. I remember my father telling us how difficult it was to take the stretchers down the bank to the various huts. He said some of them were terribly wounded. We used to see quite a few of them when they were on convalescence in their saxe-blue uniform and red ties.

Sometimes I would go with my Dad on a Sunday morning to Orpington station, where the St John's Ambulance team was

---

❛ We boys paid no attention to the news and it was only when something happened locally that we were aware of it. An anti-aircraft gun on the railway started to fire when raiders came over at night. A searchlight was stationed by the bridge from which we could watch the men practising. As the gun moved up and down the line we could be startled by an unexpectedly loud bang, more alarming than the raids, of which we took no notice.

With the Armistice in 1918, there was a great sense of relief but I do not recollect the same kind of popular celebration that followed the end of WWII. ❜

Harold Bowden of Mackenzie Road, Beckenham, born 1909, pupil at Alexandra School

---

63

based. They had first aid classes and his team won a shield. Each man was presented with a silver egg-stand with four egg cups and spoons on. It took pride of place on our dresser. I used to think it was wonderful to have boiled egg in a silver egg cup. I learned later that it was silver-plated. We had to walk home from Orpington station via Locks Bottom, where dad would buy me a lemonade and a Brighton biscuit while he had half a pint of ale, and then we walked across the fields to Balfour Road for dinner. I was always very tired when we got home.

Chatterton Road *shopping centre in the early* 20th *century catered for all the needs of the local community* (picture courtesy of Nigel Burke of William Burke and Michael Ltd Home Furnishings)

Food must have been very scarce as I remember along Chatterton Road there was a soup kitchen where we used to go and queue for pease pudding and faggots and a steamed pudding. We had to take two basins and get the first course in one and the pudding in the other. I can't remember what it was like by the time we brought it home. Then we used to go to the Home and Colonial store or Uptons or David Greig to see if there was margarine that wasn't rationed. Luckily, my grandmother [who lived at Hawkhurst] used to send us rabbits, butter and eggs from time to time. We all used to stand round the kitchen table while mother unpacked and if fruit was in season there would be apples, plums or damsons. It came in a wooden box delivered free as far as Bickley Station, but we had to pay the carter who brought it to the door.

What else do I remember of the First World War? I remember the people who used to work in the munitions factories always had an ochre look about them. Mum said it was because of the powder that they had to put in the shells and bombs.

Also we started to have buses. They were very few and far between and you used to sit on benches, six either side, with a few more seats upstairs, but there was no cover as all buses were open top. Women began to be conductors, which seemed very strange. Before this they had always stayed at home or had gone "into service". My Aunty Dolly went and worked in the Army Pay Corps and my cousin Kit went into the telephone exchange at Brixton. Telephones were just coming into use.

There was a big recruiting drive for soldiers as things were very grim and we were losing the war. So we went into Bromley Market

Drake, *the fund raising tank, was in Bromley for three days in March 1918. The streets were decorated, bands played and, with rousing speeches to spur them on, the people of Bromley bought War Bonds with a special Tank Stamp on them. The target was to raise £100,000, enough for a submarine. They raised £176,000. (BLSL)*

Square, with Mum pushing Nora in her pram, where we saw this enormous army tank. They told us all the wonderful things it could do. [The tank was in Bromley to raise money through the sale of War Bonds. See picture previous page.]

I was in school, in the top class of the infants, when we were told that the war had ended. That night all the people close to us in Balfour Road had a fireworks party. There was a gunpowder factory close by and we children went round and bought fireworks (not like today's) mostly squibs and jumping crackers. When the Peace Treaty was signed the big-wigs of Bromley gave a Peace Party. We had to take a mug with pink tape or ribbon tied to it. That was our school colour for the day. We had pink tied round our arm too. We were all to meet on the main road opposite St Luke's Church but when my mother took me there I wouldn't go as there were masses of children in a long crocodile and we had to march to the recreation ground at the bottom of Martin's Hill. However, in the evening I did go with Mum, Dad, Nora and Syd. There I had my first ride on a roundabout and swing. Of course there was lots of rejoicing everywhere because things had been so very grim during the war.

The following year, after the war had ended, we celebrated Empire Day on the 24 May. I was in the junior part of the school. We had to wear white dresses and red, white and blue hair ribbon. Our parents were invited to come and hear us all sing and I recited. We were taught that we had a wonderful empire and the sun never set on it. This is part of the song our class sang:

> *Some flags are red and white and blue*
> *And some are yellow too*
> *But the dear, dear flag that we love best*
> *Is the red, the white and the blue*

The best part of all was having a half day holiday!

[1] **Edith Cavell.** Born 4 December 1865 near Norwich, Norfolk, was executed by firing squad by the Germans in Brussels on 12 October 1915 for aiding the escape of British and French soldiers. She was buried in the prison where the execution took place. In 1919 her body was re-interred and she now lies near the main door leading into Norwich Cathedral.

[2] **Silvertown** This occurred on 19 January 1917 when about 50 tons of TNT exploded due to a fire at the munitions and chemical works of Brunner Mond at West Silvertown on the river Thames in the East End of London. A large part of the area was wrecked with over 450 casualties, including 69 killed.

[3] **Airship** 2-3 September 1916. Lt. William Leefe Robinson of the Royal Flying Corps sighted an airship over north London which was flying lower than normal; perhaps to find/sight targets. He engaged the airship with the newly fitted tracer-firing machine gun and the airship caught fire, exploded and crashed into fields in Cuffley, Hertfordshire. This night-time explosion was also seen and reported in the war diary of the Canadian Hospital in Orpington.

[4] **Chislehurst bomb crater** A newspaper cutting of 20 February 1920, about the bomb crater on Chislehurst Common, under a photo of railings, says: "The Chislehurst Conservators have enclosed, at the request of residents, the large hole on the Common where the last German bomb fell in England, on Whit Sunday, 1918. It is proposed to plant a tree in the railed enclosure."

[5] **District Ambulance Corps** The book *Orpington, From Saxon times to the Great War,* produced by the WEA after the First World War, lists members of the Orpington and District Ambulance Corps during the War and includes Nancy's father, Horace Newby.

This article is an abridged version of Nancy Tubb's reminiscences, as recorded by her daughter Rosemary Mitchell, which appeared in BBLHS magazine, Bromleage, in 2000. Additional information by the then editor, Denise Rason.

Boy Scouts *helped in the VAD hospitals as orderlies and stretcher bearers and the two pictured left were photographed at Church House, Bromley. Above, a Scout on the roof of the police station in Widmore Road, Bromley, sounds the All Clear. The Scouts were "splendid", declared the Bromley Congregational Church War History, "careering about in the small hours of the morning with their cheerful bugle calls, assuring us the raiders had been driven home". Warning of air raids was given by firing maroons next to the fire station.*
(BLSL)

Rural Schooldays

Christine Hellicar

Schooling in 1914 was a mixture of the basics — reading, writing and arithmetic — and the practical. Children often left at the age of 12 or 13 and even when they were still at school had jobs with local shopkeepers or on the farms to help out the family finances.

In rural areas the requirements of the agricultural economy had always taken precedence over education in the summer: the children were needed in the fields. The school log books for Farnborough, St Mary Cray and Chelsfield show they closed in June for the "fruiting holiday" and opened again at the end of July, only to close again in late August for another month for the "hopping vacation".

School gardens were also a part of education and they expanded during the war. The 1918 school garden report for St Mary Cray shows that 14 pupils were cultivating potatoes, onions, beet and carrots and fruit trees. In Hayes, schoolmaster William Plant — whose son was killed in 1916 — ran a boys' gardening club and each pupil had his own small allotment. In 1916 they harvested 280lb of potatoes and 200lb of onions. All the Hayes children were encouraged to pick blackberries and in September 1918 more than 160lbs of blackberries were combined with rhubarb, made into jam and sold to the parishioners.

Girls were taught practical household skills and during the war they were encouraged to knit "useful things" for the soldiers. Schools were also used to distribute leaflets on food rationing.

But there were fun times, such as a fundraising event reported by the *Orpington Times* in November 1916 when the pupils at St Mary Cray School "of their own initiative held a bazaar ... providing funds for comforts to the old boys who were fighting for their country". They raised £30.

And in the log book of Chelsfield School it was recorded: "Owing to the military parade passing the school at 12 noon, about eight children followed and thus returned too late in afternoon to receive marks. The attendance officer visited and it was reported and children warned."

In the classroom, women took more senior teaching positions as the men left for the front. At Chelsfield village school, Miss Tester took over as headmistress when headmaster George Butcher joined the Royal Flying Corps He resumed his role three years and three months later. Other teachers were often absent from school doing war work. In Farnborough, both Miss Swan and the headmistress joined the Farnborough detachment of the Red Cross Society and children were often left in the charge of young assistant teachers.

Empire Day was a highlight in the school calendar — the children had a half day's holiday. It was a day for patriotic songs such as *There's a Noble Flag* and *Obedient to the Call*. At Orpington in 1914, children from Chislehurst Road School marched to Broomhill Common and the "flag was enthusiastically saluted by the young folk". It was a day of patriotic entertainment by the children for an audience of 300 people and again fundraising.

By 1917 Empire Day was a little more subdued in Farnborough. The headmaster gave a short address calling attention to the necessity of keeping to the bread ration and to the great need for not wasting anything. After his exhortations, the National Anthem was sung and the flag saluted.

These school log books give a glimpse of children's lives but they do not mention the one thing that overshadowed every child's schooldays — the loss of a father, brother, friend or former pupil. No pupil would have been untouched.

Sources

St Mary Cray and Chelsfield School log books transcribed by Paul Rason
St Mary Cray and Orpington Times,
Farnborough Board Schools a Short History, 1973
The Story of Green Street Green, Marjorie Ford and Geoffrey Rickard
The Village School, Hayes, Jean Wilson

Empire Day *was celebrated on 24 May, Queen Victoria's birthday. It had been instituted in the UK in 1904 to "remind children that they formed part of the British Empire, and that they might think, with others in lands across the sea, what it meant to be sons and daughters of such a glorious Empire". It was also impressed upon them that "the strength of the Empire depended upon them, and they must never forget it".*

There were civic celebrations and events on local recreation grounds such as St Martin's Hill in Bromley. Empire Day celebrations are recorded in many school log books and children were given a half-day holiday.

Soldiers can be seen among the crowds in this picture outside The Railway Signal at Bromley South during a wartime Empire Day. (BLSL)

The Gilbert family*: One picture represents the grief that was suffered by so many families. In the back row, from left to right, are Alice, whose fiancé was killed; Annie, whose husband William Walker was killed; George, who died at Vimy Ridge in 1917; Edith; Harold, severely wounded; and Elsie. Seated in front of them are their parents, William and Maria. (RC)*

Letters from the Front
William, Harold and George

Ron Cox

Letters and postcards were the only form of long distance communication for ordinary families and the surviving correspondence of one Bromley family tells a tale of the tragedy that was played out in so many homes

It is frequently said that some families were devastated by World War One. This is certainly the case with the Gilbert family of Bromley. William and Maria Gilbert, who lived at 8 South Street in 1914, had six children. Of these, one daughter lost a husband and another a fiancé. One son was killed and has no known grave and the other was left for dead on the battlefield and owed his life to an unidentified medical orderly who, after dark, discovered him and brought him to safety. Only the husbands of the two youngest daughters came through unscathed as they were engaged in war work at home and exempt from fighting.

William and Annie

Harriet Marianne (Annie) Walker was the oldest child in the family and in 1912 she married gardener William Walker. They had a son the following year. William was 25 when war broke out. A letter from Annie to her parents at the end of February 1916 told them that his employers had twice written to the Recruiting Committee asking that he might be exempted from military service but, she continued: "It seems you can't do anything until the [age] group is called." Any subsequent appeal failed and William joined the 294th Siege Battery of the Royal Garrison Artillery. Before going to France he was stationed at Lydd and sent Annie four picture postcards that showed her the guns he was training on — a "French mortar", a "4.7 battery in action", and a "15-pounder in Action, showing Recoil". He added: "The guns we were firing with

Training in Lydd*: William Walker sent his wife Annie picture postcards of the artillery they were being taught to use. Above, a Trench Mortar, and, below, a card captioned "15-Pounder In Action (Showing Recoil) R.A. Lydd". William wrote: "The guns we were training with this week." He went straight to the front and three months later was dead (RC)*

this week." The fourth reads: "6-Inch Howitzer in Action", on which he wrote: "The gun we fire next."

Those of us who served in World War II would have found it somewhat bizarre to send picture postcards of a 17-pounder gun, or a Sherman tank, or a .30 cal Browning machine gun. It shows, perhaps, a deep-seated difference between the mentality of both soldier and civilian in the two wars.

Less than three months later, William was dead. He was killed in action on Thursday 21 March, on the first day of the German Spring Offensive. He is interred at Fins New British Cemetery at Sorel-le Grand, between Cambrai and Peronne.

A draft copy remains, in the family archives, of a letter that widow Annie must have written to William's commanding officer:

> "I have received your letter telling me of my dear husband's death and I thank you for writing to tell me, and for your sympathy ... I have not heard from the War Office yet.
> I should very much like to know if the funeral was able to take place. I should like to feel he was laid to rest and if it's possible for a photo of his grave to be sent to me. I should be very grateful but after the terrible news in the papers I feel this may be much to expect.
> "My husband's father and mother both wish to thank you for your sympathy ... he was indeed a good husband and a good son and we feel his loss acutely ... I should be comforted to know he did not suffer, if this is so.
> "Thanking you again for your kindness and I should be grateful if you could write to me again.
> "I remain yours truly ..."

There is a picture of the grave in the family archive.

Harold

Annie's brother Harold, had left school at 14 to join the Bromley and Cray Gas Company as an office boy. He had already been in and out of France when William was killed. He had survived, but only just. When only 17, he had falsified his age and joined the 18th Battalion, Royal Fusiliers. He seems to have been one of a number of employees of the South Suburban Gas Company who joined up.

More than 50 letters survive that Harold wrote home between November 1915, when he was about to embark for France, and July 1916, when he returned home severely wounded. They all show his humour, his adaptability and his interest in food. Just before he embarked he wrote (very optimistically as it transpired): "I think that Germany is beginning to feel the pinch and nothing in the nature of a sudden collapse would surprise me ... I've had my hair cropped; it feels A1. The Colonel made us practice a march past, the other afternoon and made a shocking fuss about it."

Soon, if not already, his unit had moved to Jellalabad Barracks, Tidworth, where, with surprising foresight, they were equipped with winter clothing — "flannelette body belt, thick wool undervest, 1 pair thick woollen [sic] gloves, gas helmet ... soft trench cap with a big flap to pull over our ears, 3 pairs socks and a new pair of puttees ... .I shall be as warm as toast ... My body belt goes round me nearly twice ... I have two thick woolen [sic] shirts, and a thick cardigan, my tunic and a thick great coat and wear 2 pairs socks and a thick pair of pants ... P.S. We have painted all our buttons black [after the belated realisation that polished buttons gave away a man's position, a lesson that had to be re-learned in World War II]."

Armed with 120 rounds of ammunition and provided with a blanket, clean shirt and pants and a clean change in his pack, and plenty of "smokes and eatables", he entrained at Tidworth. "The lads," he wrote, "are as lively as larks and there is a lot of singing going on and everyone is trying to make more noise than anyone else."

By January 1916 Harold had been in and out of the trenches several times, though the mind boggles at the thought of his marching not only with rifle, pack, gas mask, ammunition, blanket and perhaps entrenching equipment, but also with a pillow (sent by his parents) and a portable cooker (for which refills had been sent by his sister Elsie).

He seems at this stage to have been in a quiet part of the Front, "quite clean after some of the Trenches we have occupied". Food from home was welcomed: apples, oranges, cake sandwich, biscuits, chocolate and bloater paste, besides tobacco and cigarettes. His parents and all his sisters were feeding him up and, on one occasion, he wrote: "I'm going to have a feed tea time. I almost tremble to think of my poor digestive organs ... I'm going to have the feed and take the consequences like a man." He often used the word "comfy" to describe his situation — probably bearing in mind his parents' and sisters' anxieties.

The Gas Company sent him a letter telling him that his salary of £5 was to be increased and he noted that the Secretary had crossed out "Dear Sir" and changed it to "Dear Gilbert".

Harold Gilbert: *formal portraits of young men in uniform would have been on nearly every mantelpiece in the land. (RC)*

All in all, he was enjoying the experience. "I had the pleasure today of seeing a German aeroplane strafed by our anti-aircraft guns," he wrote. "It was jolly interesting."

Rumours abounded about the enemy being slaughtered, though none similar about the Allies. Hence such comments as on 1 February 1916: "It won't be many weeks I think before we come home — not on leave — but for good." Meantime, he was in and out of the trenches, the weather was "fairly decent" and, for nearly a week, he was in an unspecified town, billeted in a "decent" empty house. "I was able to buy a good many things ... went to a concert given by various men in our Division."

But just occasionally, the veil slips. "We had rather a lively bombardment the first day we were [back] in [the trenches]. One chap was hit. It lasted for three hours so I went to the Sergeant's dug-out which was right underground until Fritz had got over his excitement. Our artillery sent them a few presents — my word they must have been large shells for they simply roared through the air."

The last two weeks of February saw him in hospital at Choques with influenza. However, he was keen to return to his unit because of the expectation that food parcels would await him. It is clear that the biggest boost to morale was the arrival of supplements to army food, sent by parents and siblings despite ever-increasing food shortages in the United Kingdom.

He became a machine-gunner. He enjoyed the training for this but said that he stood little chance of winning the Victoria Cross as he thought the war would be over too soon. A sign of this, he believed, was that they had returned to polishing their buttons.

Harold's existence, until after Easter [1916], was of a serenity that one never associates with life on the Western Front. His billet was at a large farm with horses, cows and five pigs "which I am getting fond of".

The people at the farm were "very homelike", the old lady was "very kind" and the daughters were "nice ... they are all over 30".

But there was a considerable element of deception. "I have just seen Sunday papers", he wrote, "and the news is cheering. I cannot imagine what the enemy are doing when they sacrifice all those men. I'm convinced [it] is the last thrust on their part."

On Easter Saturday Harold again expressed the view that "the war is going to end soon and then I am coming home to stay. I often think that these few months that I have been in the army have not actually been wasted ... I am not in the least danger".

But the very next day, all that changed. Harold was posted to the 8th Royal Fusiliers and, as he forecast "I shall soon be in the

Trenches again." There followed weeks of training.

At this point his letters show two changes. One, he asks his parents to get their doctor to write to Colonel Annersley asking if he can have leave (a) on account of their poor health and (b) because "I'm a kid", but the latter was unlikely to have much effect, even though he had enlisted under age, because he had been in France for seven months without the matter being raised.

Second, by mid-June his unit was constantly being moved about and by night he was often working in the trenches, carrying "big lumps of planks about for dug-outs". On one night he was out in the rain for seven hours making his rifle "red with rust" and "difficult to clean". There followed a march and a train journey to Amiens. From there, he wrote home on 15 June what was to be his last letter for a month. The next came from a hospital in Rouen after he had been wounded.

The Somme

The battle of the Somme extended over the Picardy plateau, north and south of the river. The small section set aside for Harold's unit was within an area just north of the Somme. By the end of the first day of the offensive, 1 July, the 4th Army had been massacred, two Divisions being decimated within an hour of the start. Over 60% of the officers and other ranks of one Division had become casualties.

The next day the sun shone on thousands of fly-blown, rotting bodies. However, Haig ordered the offensive to continue. But before that could be done the battlefield had to be cleared of the wounded. Harold's Division was one of two now brought forward to replace those that had been destroyed and, as he later recorded, 2 and 3 July were occupied in fatigues, in other words cleaning up the battlefield ready for the next massacre; truly, an example of digging one's own grave.

On the 4th, heavy showers flooded the trenches and made some crumble. More dead and wounded were brought back in. Next day, there were further massive losses on both sides.

At 8.26 am on 7 July, Harold's Company went "over the top" and lay out in the open. The weather was bad and, although no rain had fallen during the night, the fumes of gas shells were blanketed in the hollows As they had left their trenches, devastating machine gun fire mowed down many, but the remainder went forward, carried on by the advance of the second and third lines.

Of the three battalions involved on this front, 91% of the officers and 83% of the other ranks had become casualties by the end of the day. Harold wrote, laconically, in his later notes: "Wounded in action. Rescued at night." He had got within 50 yards of the German defences before being hit. He was wounded in the ankle, the right arm and, badly, in the back. He lay on the ground, not expecting to see the light of day. But a young orderly, scouting for signs of life, found him and brought him in. Harold never knew who it was, but that man saved his life.

From a casualty clearing station he was moved to hospital in Rouen, in a dangerous condition. Yet, he was still buoyant. "I am getting on very well," he wrote (or, rather, dictated), "there is nothing serious or complicated but only that which a little time will put right ... It was jolly good fun going over the top — my only regret being that a machine gun stopped my progress 50 yards from their line thus preventing once more Fritz and myself getting too familiar". Army Form B104-80 was sent out by the Infantry Record Office to notify his family 12 days after his injury, but was wrongly addressed and reached his parents after a further 12 days. Even then, his wound was wrongly described as being in the chest.

Five days later, he was back in England and able to send a characteristically cheerful letter. "I am going on famously," he dictated. He tells his parents of his arm and ankle injuries but makes no mention of the serious wound on his left side which resulted in the removal of 13cm of rib cage and half of one lung. He remained in hospital for 11 months.

He was honourably discharged on 8 August 1917, 27 months after he had first enlisted, having spent nearly half that time in hospital. Shortly, he returned to the South Suburban Gas Company's Works (at Sydenham), a wiser, more mature, less robust, man. His main wound continued to trouble him for the rest of his life (his wife often had to plug the hole when it suppurated).

He appreciated the fact of his survival and was highly regarded, both in his family and at work, for his interest in, and support of, those around him, especially if they needed help.

George

George, 20, was a Smith's bookstall manager at Bromley North railway station in 1914. He was a much more reluctant soldier than his brother Harold. Although four years older, born 1893, he initially sought deferment but was called up in April 1916. He had had a medical in October 1914, when he was a quite hefty 5ft 10in tall and weighed 11 stone four pounds. He joined the 2/5 Battalion of the Bedfordshire Regiment.

No correspondence survives. George was not a great communicator and he seems to have had none of the youthful enthusiasm of his younger brother.

By 14 December 1916 (when Harold had been back in England in hospital for five months) George embarked at Folkestone for France. He had been posted to the 1st Battalion, the Bedfordshire Regiment.

But for George, things were much nastier than they had been for Harold. Two battalions from each Brigade were put into the front line, and one in support and one in reserve at Bethune, relief happening every four or five days. Many of the communication trenches had between 15 and 30cm of water in them and, in some, even small fish were to be seen.

During this time, improved gas helmets were issued and "trench feet" was alleviated by the issue of "gum boots". There was a hard frost for three weeks (skin coats were issued) and there was much snow. Both sides were exhausted and, what activity there was, comprised sniping, trench-mortaring and an occasional foray by raiding parties.

George's 15th Brigade was assigned to attack Vimy Ridge. A Field Service Card, sent to George's parents, indicates that he had already been wounded. But, unfortunately, it wasn't a "Blighty" and so he had returned to his unit. Five days later, on Easter Sunday, he wrote his last letter home. Unfortunately, his letters were not only less frequent than Harold's, they were also less interesting and less informative.

The battle for Vimy Ridge began on Easter Monday (9 April) and the greater part of the Ridge was speedily captured. At that moment, George was not involved and was bivouacked in woods. He found time to send several field cards on which printed options could be deleted or not, and on the 21st he sent what was to be his final message. He left, undeleted "1 am quite well" and "Letter follows at first opportunity". This card and other earlier ones, his mother put in an envelope marking it "The last letter, envelope

NOTHING is to be written on this side except the date and signature of the sender. Sentences not required may be erased. If anything else is added the post card will be destroyed.

[Postage must be prepaid on any letter or post card addressed to the sender of this card.]

I am quite well.

I have been admitted into hospital

{ sick } and am going on well.
{ wounded } and hope to be discharged soon.

I am being sent down to the base.

I have received your { letter dated _____
{ telegram ,, _____
{ parcel ,, _____

Letter follows at first opportunity.

I have received no letter from you

{ lately
{ for a long time.

Signature }
only }

Date_____

W¹ W1566 R1619-18539 8000m. 6-17. C & Co., Grange Mills, S.W

Field Service Card: Many young men such as George Gilbert were not great letter writers and their communications to their families were often these pre-printed forms. One surviving from George says "I am quite well", "I have received your parcel" and "Letter follows at first opportunity" — but no letters survive. (MR)

82

IN LOVING MEMORY OF

George William Gilbert,

The dearly loved son of George & Maria Gilbert,

Killed in Action at Vimy Ridge.
April 23rd, 1917.

———

"GREATER LOVE HATH NO MAN."

In Memoriam cards *were sent by the family to friends and relations. The following verse was printed on the left hand side:*

> Somewhere in France they have laid him.
> Somewhere in France he fell:
> How little we thought when we parted,
> It would be our last farewell

destroyed, and Field Card received from my son 33010 Pte GW Gilbert 1st Batt Beds Regiment".

The Second Battle of the Scarpe began on 23 April, and somewhere between 4.45am and 3pm on, ironically, St George's Day, George Gilbert was killed. George was initially reported missing and the *Daily Sketch* of 8 August, under the heading "Ten missing men: friends are asking for news", listed George (with photo).

So far as is known, there was no response and on 21 January 1918 his father received a letter, rubber-stamped "RW Maxwell, Major, for Colonel, Officer-in-Charge Records". It read:

> *"Sir. It is my painful duty to inform you that no further news having been received of 33010 Pte G W Gilbert ... the Army Council have been regretfully constrained to conclude that he is dead ...*

"I am to express to you the sympathy of the Army Council with you in your loss.

"Any articles of private property which are found will be forwarded to this Office, but they cannot be disposed of until authority is received from the War Office. Application regarding the disposal of any such personal effects addressed to The Secretary, The War Office and marked, outside/Effects.

"I am. Sir, your Obedient Servant."

With curt formality, almost a year after his death, his father received a detailed statement of accounts and £3-8s-6d, this being the balance due to George after deduction, for example, of 2s-4d for National Insurance.

There followed a beautifully-written Scroll of Remembrance with two printed cover notes (from Lord Derby, Secretary of State for War, and from the King and Queen), his British War Medal and a Victory War Medal, a bronze memorial plaque from the King.

To what extent these pieces of paper and metal were a comfort, it is impossible to say. On the one hand they must have reopened wounds of distress and grief; on the other, they were a tangible reminder of someone young who had been killed unnecessarily. Having no known grave, George is commemorated by name in Bay 5 of the Arras Memorial.

This was just one family but their personal tragedy fleetingly captured in personal and official documents was repeated in homes everywhere.

Bibliography

Gilbert family archives

Census returns 1881-1911

Correspondence: Royal Artillery Historical Trust

Edmonds, JE, *History of the Great War Military Operations, France and Belgium, 1918,* 1935

Falls, Cyril, *History of the Great War ... Military Operations, France and Belgium,* 1917

Farndale, Sir Martin, *History of the Royal Regiment of Artillery: Western France 1914-1918,* 1986

GRO, Birth, Marriage and Death certificates

Gladden, Norman, *The Somme* 1916: *A Personal Account, 1974*

Hockley, Farrar-, AH, *The Somme*,1983

Hussey, A H & Inman, DS, *The Fifth Division in the Great War,1921*

Hutchison, Graham Seton, *The Thirty-Third Division in France and Flanders,* 1915-1918, 1921

Maurice, Sir F, *The 16th Foot: A History of the Bedfordshire and Hertfordshire Regiment,* 1936

Middlebrook, Martin & Mary, *The Somme Battlefields,* 1994

O'Neill, H C, *The Royal Fusiliers in the Great War, 1922*

Scott, Sir Arthur B (ed), *History of the 12th (Eastern) Division in the Great War, 1914-1918,* 1921

The Somme, Vol 1: The First Battle of the Somme (1916-1917), Michelin, 1919

George Gilbert's name is one of thousands on the Arras and other memorials in Belgium and France that commemorate those who have no known grave

An army of nurses

*At the outbreak of war Annie Walker,
whose family features in the previous
article, became a VAD nurse. Like many
of the young women who served in the
hospitals, she was soon to become a
widow. (RC)*

Caring for the Casualties

Joyce Walker

The core of Red Cross work in the war was provided by male and female Voluntary Aid Detachments (VADs) who supplemented the nursing and ambulance services of the Territorial Forces.
VADs had to possess First Aid and Nursing Certificates and be trained to make use of local resources, for the improvisation of stretchers, for methods of transport and for converting local buildings into hospitals and rest stations for the sick and wounded.

The inaugural meeting of the Bromley Division of the Kent Branch of the British Red Cross Society was held in Bromley Public Library, on 28 April 1910. In October, the secretary Dr Yolland wrote to the Council asking for the loan of certain buildings for use as temporary hospitals in a time of national emergency.

A report in the *Bromley Archives* records that the Mayor said it was only in the very improbable event of an *invasion* (laughter) — that the buildings would be required. He thought it such an improbable, although not an impossible event, it would be the duty of everyone to afford every facility they possibly could for the nursing of the sick and wounded ("hear, hear").

The Mayor was not alone in his reaction to the request, wherever offers of help were sought they were given without hesitation, but talk of war provoked "hoots of laughter", according to Mrs Nellie Barker, who was a Beckenham VAD.

Nevertheless, despite amused reactions, ladies' and men's detachments were formed in the Bromley Division, a Division which covered much of the area now administered by the London Borough of Bromley.

The detachments, when registered, were each given a number with a "Kent" prefix — the ladies' were given even numbers the men odd. One of the first ladies' detachments formed in Bromley was registered as Kent 50 and covered the area of Bromley

Common, Keston and Hayes. Lady Lubbock of High Elms arranged classes in her home and it was there that the very first VADs qualified.

There were six other detachments in Bromley, three in Beckenham and others in West Wickham, Shortlands, Chislehurst, Farnborough and Orpington. The volunteers gained their training in local and London hospitals.

The numbers in the men's detachments fluctuated quite considerably as men joined the colours or, as in the case of railway employees during the war, were debarred from active participation by reason of diminished staff. Nevertheless, the detachments were able to keep up their numbers with those unfit, over-age or ineligible for military service and with those attested and waiting call. There were two men's detachments in Bromley — one a St John's Ambulance Company, prior to the organisation of the county scheme. Beckenham provided two detachments.

In many respects, the men had a harder task before the war, by virtue of the fact that they were working during the day and so had to undertake their Red Cross training in their spare time. Whereas the ladies were, in the main, according to Miss Helena Harrison, a Beckenham VAD, "living at home helping mother or perhaps doing a little social work". The men were expected to attend training sessions even during the war.

Field Days were a regular feature of the men's training schedules and one such recorded in the *Beckenham Journal* was held at Layhams Farm, West Wickham, by the Beckenham detachment in 1915. "It was a very hot day as the men set off from the Croydon Road Recreation Ground at some time after 10 o'clock, visibly uncomfortable in their high collars. Their fine marching was marred in Beckenham High Street when they became entangled with a boys' band out on a marching exercise. After sorting out the men from the boys, the instruments from the first aid bags and the stretchers, the detachment, undeterred, marched on.

"Good time was made in reaching West Wickham, where it encountered the Clapham Volunteer Corps whose members were en route from Crystal Palace to Keston. The peace and quiet of the village was shattered by the bustle of passing vehicles, the footpaths were crowded with civilians, members of the Clapham VTC and the merry men of Kent 39. Some of the old folk were of the opinion that the Huns had come at last!"

The ladies, too, had their Field Days, making good use of Hayes Common on several occasions. Camping also formed part of their training and on Saturday 2 August 1913, a week's camp for 170 Kent VADs was held at Broomfield Hall, Herne, with the 1st Gravesend Boy Scouts standing guard duty and acting as orderlies and patients. A small group of Regular and Territorial Medical Officers and Instructors helped with training in first aid, catering, cooking, construction of field ovens, semaphore, and an understanding of the necessity of a pure water supply, proper sanitation and the disposal of refuse. It must have been very exciting for many of the campers who "only helped mother", to engage in such activities.

In 1914 another camp was held at Rolvenden, when, according to Dr Rex Yolland of Bickley, "it rained nearly all the time". Despite the obvious difficulties, the exercise proved very successful, all the

Stretcher bearers at the training camp at Rolvenden
(BLSL, Joyce Walker collection)

more valuable as camp was struck just 10 days before Britain declared war on Germany on 4 August 1914.

The casualties arrive

During 1914 preparations for mobilisation had been proceeding apace and many private houses, halls, equipment and funds were promised by local residents

On the evening of Tuesday 13 October 1914, just after 10 o'clock, the telephone rang in the headquarters of the Kent Red Cross at 53 Bromley Common. A telegram was read out from the GPO: "Mobilise all your hospitals at once. Notify names of places, stations and numbers of beds available at each to transport officers, Folkestone. Large number of wounded arrive tonight. Authority Director-General AMS Colonel Wilson, SMO."

Fatigue was forgotten as carefully laid plans were set in motion and telephone messages went out all over Kent via the solitary telephone operator on night duty at the Bromley Exchange.

It took several hours before all detachments were mobilised and even then, because much of the equipment consisted of promises on paper, private individuals had to be roused from their slumbers. There was much to-ing and fro-ing and owners of private cars were pressed into service, as well as business vans.

One prominent citizen of Keston, Mr JW Wheeler-Bennett, found himself briefly suspected of being a burglar while doing some knocking-up!

At noon on 14 October the first convoy of wounded was detrained at Bromley South Station by members of the Bromley detachments, who then transported them to the auxiliary hospitals which by some miracle of organisation were ready for their patients. One immediate problem, not foreseen, was the language difficulty — most of the first arrivals were Belgian — but, like all other problems, it simply melted away.

Bromley had 11 auxiliary hospitals ready. These included schools, church halls and houses with 252 beds ranging from a house in Hayes Road with four beds to St Mary's Church Hall, Plaistow, with 65 beds.

Orders to mobilise the Chislehurst detachments were received at midnight on 13 October, and Christ Church Hall with 25 beds was ready for occupation by 6am the next day. The first convoy of 33 Belgians was received at 9am. A second convoy of 30 Belgians arrived on 17 October and were housed at Abbey Lodge.

The second Chislehurst detachment, on receiving its orders to mobilise, took over Holbrook House, scrubbed and fitted it up with 35 beds by 5am, four hours before 35 Belgians arrived. On 16 October, Holbrook House was also taken into use with 50 beds and an operating theatre. Among the Chislehurst VADs was a young lady who rejoiced in the name of Florence Nightingale.

West Wickham had four hospitals, of which only two were used on that fateful 14 October — The Warren (55 beds) and Coney Hall (seven beds). Later on, Hayes Grove in Prestons Road was brought into service with 20 beds.

Orpington Village Hall, *below left, was the main VAD hospital in the village. The first soldiers, 66 wounded Belgians, arrived on14 October 1914. Nearly 1,500 patients were treated during the war and there were no fatalities. Members of the VAD unit are pictured, top left, in their formal uniforms. The Village Hall was demolished in 1968 and replaced by the Templegate shops and offices to the left of the covered entrance to The Walnuts shopping centre. (BLSL)*

Wounded Belgian soldiers at Abbey Lodge, Chislehurst:
_many of the large Victorian houses in Chislehurst were
hurriedly converted in 1914 to become hospitals run by the
VAD. The Chislehurst Detachment was known as Kent 60 and
Christchurch Parish Hall in Lubbock Road was the receiving
centre._

_In October 1914 Abbey Lodge — Chislehurst Hall as it is
now known — which had been empty for some time, became
a convalescent hospital run by Miss Beatrix Batten. Beatrix,
the daughter of a Christ Church churchwarden, received a
CBE from the Queen in 1955 to mark her lifelong dedication to
the Red Cross._

_Several houses in Lubbock Road were used as hospitals,
the sanatorium of Coed Bel School for Girls, now Willow
Lodge, St Hugh's school, formerly Lamas, the home of Sir
John Lubbock, and Brooklyn. Further information can be
found on the Lost Hospitals of London website at
www.ezitis.myzen.co.uk/_ (JF)

Beckenham was no less generous — the Christ Church Schools were converted overnight into a 50-bed military hospital, Orpington's detachment set up its hospital of 30 beds in the Village Hall and on 14 October another temporary hospital at St Mary Cray. The trustees of the Wesleyan Church in Farnborough made their church available to the Red Cross detachment who, at 12 hours notice, opened its hospital there with 17 beds on 16 October.

The response to the original telegram from Colonel Wilson was magnificent; overnight nearly 500 beds had been made ready. All the hours given over to training had been vindicated and all members set to with enthusiasm. The ladies worked full or part-time according to their circumstances, in the wards, kitchen, office, linen-room, wherever their talents were needed. The gentlemen worked as ambulance drivers, stretcher-bearers, orderlies and the local doctors who found themselves in charge of the hospitals were able to call on the services of many eminent specialists who lived in and around the Bromley area.

The Lady Superintendents of the detachments became the Matrons, assisted in each case by one or two trained nurses, not all of whom claimed their salary. In the case of the VADs who, of course, were not paid, 2s-6d [12½p] a week was allowed for laundry.

The majority of the soldiers received in the first few days were suffering from rheumatism, some had bullet wounds and others shrapnel wounds. As the war progressed, the patients sent to auxiliary hospitals were generally, but not invariably, those suffering from less-serious wounds or ailments, or those in need of convalescence. Much depended on the war situation, for when the big battles were being fought, the military hospitals were overwhelmed and without the Red Cross hospitals and ambulance services, the system would have broken down.

All the auxiliary hospitals were attached to military hospitals and in this area they were the Royal Herbert Hospital, the Brook War Hospital, the Ontario Hospital, Orpington, and the Queen's Facial Hospital at Frognal, Sidcup.

In 1915 a 50-bed hospital was opened at Oakley House,

Balgowan School, Beckenham: *built in 1914, it became a hospital as soon as the building work finished. Initially the hospital had 100 beds but, with the addition of two marquees, the accommodation was eventually increased to 240 beds, making it the largest auxiliary hospital in the area.*

Fourteen medics got together to provide their own transport for the hospitals in Beckenham and this picture is believed to show some of those medics, along with men from the VAD Kent 41,with the ambulance they provided. Dr George Robert Fabris Stilwell, the Commandant, is on the right in the picture and standing on the far side of the car is Dr Tim Randall.

The people of Beckenham provided all the equipment, including X-ray, for Christ Church, Balgowan and other Beckenham buildings to be turned into hospitals.

Gifts at Christmas 1915 to Balgowan include 24 hot-water bottles, 100 treasure bags, operating table and medical bags, dressing gowns, bed tables and lockers, books, concert proceeds, entire covering of floors with lino. From local schools came 134 tumblers, ash trays, handkerchiefs, cigarettes , china, cocoa, and shaving equipment.

During the war the hospital cared for 5,257 Eastern Command soldiers, the largest number of casualties for any VAD hospital in Bromley. A memorial commemorating the role of the school during this period is located in the main school hall. (BLSL)

Bromley Common, equipped with an operating theatre and X-ray apparatus, replacing three of the Bromley hospitals. Another 20 beds were added in 1916 which were later set aside for the use of patients from the Queen's Facial Hospital.

Also in 1915, in Bromley, five more of the original hospitals were closed when a Mr Medcalf offered Elstree, 41 Westmoreland Road, for use as a hospital. It was particularly well situated for the ambulance trains arriving at Bromley South Station. Further beds were provided in Bromley in September 1915 when Church House was equipped and opened as a hospital of some 50 beds. Two months later, yet another hospital was opened in Springhill, Bromley, a Domestic Economy School lent by the Kent Education Committee, and equipped with 38 beds (later increased to 43) and an operating theatre.

All this activity was being repeated elsewhere as bigger hospitals began to replace some of the initial smaller sites. In Beckenham, Kelsey Cottage had been opened in November 1914 with 51 beds — a particularly beautiful and peaceful setting for a hospital. In November 1915, Beckenham Urban District Council lent the Balgowan Road School, which became the biggest hospital in the area with 240 beds, (see picture on opposite page) and Kelsey Cottage was returned to its owner.

Other properties in Shortlands and West Wickham closed but the VADs continued to work in other hospitals in Beckenham and Bromley, in needlework depots and canteens, while two VADs went to France and another to Egypt.

So much for statistics. Behind them lay hours of hard work, problems, pride, tears and laughter. Perhaps a memory recalled by Miss Helena Harrison would bring some life to the figures: "When batches of wounded arrived, dirty and exhausted, straight from the front, there would be a hectic hour getting them clean and to bed. Then the doctor would start his rounds while junior nurses held bowls or acted in some minor capacity. We saw enough to realise what war meant as septic wounds and frostbites were uncovered and men winced under the doctor's gentle probing. If you felt 'quee' in those early unhardened days (some of us were only 18), you slipped ashamedly out of the ward and pulled yourself

Warren House, West Wickham, *was a hospital for a short time early in the war and the women pictured above are in the kitchen. When not nursing, there were plenty of practical jobs to be done, such as rolling bandages and making slippers for wounded soldiers. Below, the slipper room at Oakley House. The goods went to a depot in Plaistow Lane, supplying the whole of Kent. (BLSL, Joyce Walker collection)*

together, probably in the stoke-hole, where no one saw if you did put your head between your knees.

"Most girls could face even operations with equanimity after a few months' training. Sometimes we nurses were terribly rushed, there was so much to do for helpless patients. Septic wounds were common, and this meant arm and leg baths going continually which had to be kept at a certain temperature. When there was a lull and our patients were convalescing, we used to help them get up evening concerts, hurrying through our duties so as to join them in the popular chorus songs of that day."

The patients themselves were appreciative of the care given them. A letter written to the *Beckenham Journal* by a Sergeant of the 1st Battalion of the 60th Rifles, a patient at The Warren, West Wickham, expresses something of that appreciation: "... Doctor Blake, who has a soldier's welfare at heart ... goodness only knows how many a poor man would be short of a limb today were it not for the doctor's skill, patience and attention. Not only have we such a clever doctor, but the Matron, Miss Maxwell, and Sister Burke-Close and their little staff of nurses work like trojans from early morning until late at night with ever-smiling faces. They not only put clean dressings on our wounds, but roll up their sleeves and scrub floors."

The boys in blue [patients who were mobile wore special blue uniforms] became a familiar sight on the streets and many were taken out for rides, excursions and picnics. A sports day was organised for them on Beckenham Cricket Club's ground, concerts were given for and on behalf of the patients, weekly egg collections were made, help was given with the modest gardens started by the convalescent patients, sports and games equipment were donated, as were gifts at Christmas — all manner of help was given by local residents.

The war ground on until the Armistice was declared on 11 November 1918. The war to end war was over, but the hospitals still functioned, mending and healing the sick and wounded. Indeed, during the influenza epidemic of 1918-19, serious cases, which could not be accepted at the Herbert Hospital, were sent direct to the Christ Church Hospital in Beckenham.

Patients at *Warren House, Coney Hall, right. The grand house — now the Metropolitan Police sports club — was owned by Sir Robert Laidlaw, MP. Not only did he make Warren House available but also gave a weekly allowance of £25 for running costs,*

equipped a theatre and provided five servants and all the produce from the garden. It closed in 1916, the year after Sir Robert died. A slightly less grand, but possibly more functional, hospital was at Cator Park Church. The main ward is pictured below. (BLSL, Joyce Walker collection)

Both Balgowan and Christ Church hospitals treated large numbers of outpatients — discharged soldiers, troops on leave and troops stationed in the locality. There were 19 hospitals in the borough by 1918 and figures for 14 of them show they treated over 22,000 patients. It was not until 31 December 1919 that the last of the Red Cross Hospitals was closed. The members of the Kent Red Cross were officially demobilised in May 1919 and to mark the occasion a Thanksgiving Service, followed by a reception, was held in the Central Hall, Bromley. More than 1,400 members attended the impressive ceremonies presided over by Marquis Camden, Lord Lieutenant of Kent.

There were to be many awards. A CBE [Commander of the British Empire] was awarded to Dr Yolland, and to others went OBEs [Order of the British Empire] and MBEs [Member of the British Empire], as well as ARRCs [Associate of the Royal Red Cross] and RRCs, [Royal Red Cross]. But perhaps the patients themselves would agree with the comment in *The Way of the Red Cross* that "the term VAD has become an honourable one and is in itself an order of distinguished service".

This is an abridged version of the late Joyce Walker's article The British Red Cross in the Bromley area 1910-1919, first published in Bromley Local History No.4 in 1979

Sources

Red Cross Archives
The British Red Cross in Action, Dame Beryl Oliver
The British Red Cross Society , Dermot Morrah.
Kent's Care for the Wounded , Paul Creswick,
G Stanley Pond & PH Ashton
The Way of the Red Cross, EC Vivian & J Hodder Williams
Beckenham Journal and *Bromley Record*
Personal recollections of Miss H Harrison, Mrs N Barker, Miss I Gill, Mrs G Thompson (née Lennard) and Dr Rex Yolland
St John's Parish Magazine, West Wickham

Hast Hill, Hayes, *became an annexe for the Canadian hospital set up at Bromley Park Hotel (now Bromley Court Hotel) in 1915. There were two small wards, which were described by the commanding officer as "large bright apartments, one with a northern and one with a southern exposure. They are on the ground floor divided from each other by a corridor, leading off which is a lavatory and bath accommodation. They each contain five beds with a square footage of about 70 feet per bed. The rooms are suitably furnished and each bed provided with a locker bedside table. In one [room] there is a dining table for the use of patients, in the other a large glass cupboard furnished with surgical dressings, etc. The house is well situated on high land and is surrounded by pleasant grounds, which patients would be allowed to use". The house still stands, converted into luxury flats. (JW)*

Coping with Tragedy
The village of Hayes

Jean Wilson

O n the declaration of war in August 1914 there was a rush by eager young men to volunteer, including more than 71 from a possible 130 from Hayes. The effect on those left in the village is hard to imagine. Every mother and wife who waved goodbye to their sons and husbands dreaded the knock on the door and the arrival of the telegram saying "We regret to inform you that your son/husband is dead".

Such a message was received by the schoolmaster William Plant and his wife Eliza in 1915, announcing that their youngest son Frederic, pictured below, had been killed at the Battle of Loos.

Frederic was a second lieutenant with 1st Battalion Royal West Surrey Regiment and had been home for a week at the beginning of September when he had become engaged. Unfortunately, he was killed a few days after his return to the front. His parents received many letters of condolence. His commanding officer, Major LM Crofts, wrote that Frederic:

"was leading his men up a communication trench leading from the German first line trench, which we had captured, when a German bomb exploded and hit him in the head, and the men near say he must have been killed at once, though no one saw him afterwards ... lack of bombs forced the men to retire to our original line, and all the wounded and dead had to be abandoned. Your son was killed leading his men in a gallant manner. His sterling qualities had made him a

favourite with all and his loss will be deeply felt in the battalion".

Mrs Plant, like many mothers, found it very difficult to come to terms with the death of her much loved youngest child, especially as nobody had survived who had witnessed the moment of his death.

Frederic was one of six former pupils of the village school who were among those remembered at a memorial service held in the Parish Church in November 1916. This may have helped the Plants and the other families in their sorrow but the loss was great. Every year Mrs Plant inserted in the local paper an "in memoriam" entry for Frederic. She also had the worry of two other sons, Ronald and Harold, who were fighting on the Western Front, but fortunately they returned safely to Hayes.

One of the youngest casualties *was 16-year-old midshipman Norman Harris of The White House, Hayes Common. He was training at the Royal Naval College at Dartmouth when war broke out. On 4 August Norman joined the old battleship HMS Bulwark, which blew up on 26 November when it was loading ammunition at Sheerness, Kent. His distraught mother never recovered from the loss of her son, which was said to be contributory to her early death in 1916.*

It was not only parents who suffered the loss. From the letters of Private Arthur Robson we read that in the same forward movement on 25 September in which Frederic Plant lost his life a German sniper killed the boyfriend of Eva Batten, a housemaid at Hayes Place, home of Sir Everard Hambro. Her three brothers were also soldiers. Ernest and Albert, who was awarded the Military Medal in February 1917, survived. Walter, however, was killed on 9 April 1917 shortly after he had been recommended for the Distinguished Conduct Medal because *"with six others he threw many thousands of bombs [grenades] all day because of the difficulty in getting ammunition up"* to the guns.

Apart from the stress and strain caused by having loved ones involved in the fighting whether on land or sea the villagers also had to cope with the effect of the departure of the most able-bodied from their community. Farmers struggled with the loss of labour as they sought to bring in their crops and in 1916 a special meeting was held to encourage women to join the newly set-up Women's National Land Service Corps. Many Hayes women were already playing an active role as members of the VAD or caring for Belgian refugees or wounded soldiers in their homes. Many of the wounded soldiers who were brought back on trains to Bromley South in 1914 and 1915 were allocated to the different temporary hospitals that were set up in the area.

By the time the war ended, 39 Hayes men had been killed in action but 103 were recorded as returning home safely. Special concerts were held to welcome the returning soldiers. However, it was not the end of the difficulties for many families. There were further deaths in 1920 from injuries or infections caused by the war, such as those of Harold Williams and Henry Brown, who died from blood poisoning caused by his time in the trenches. Many had been affected by their war experiences. Some were unsettled and could no longer remain in the village and others had injuries that limited their chance of work.

Charlie Harrod, who fought with 8 Battalion Yorkshire Regiment, was wounded in the leg in France in 1917. He was discharged from the army in 1918 because of his disability. He

One of the smallest villages in Bromley, *Hayes was a farming community with a population of around 1000. The village centre was at Hayes Street, where many of the old buildings have survived, but there were also farms and big houses scattered around the parish. Pictured above, tilling at Hayes Place Farm. Below, the Northern end of West Common Road, Hayes, in the early 20th century with Bank Cottages, the Village School and the Forge on the left. Myrtle Cottage, on the right, was at the end of the "island site", situated between West Common Road and Baston Road, and was later demolished. (JW)*

always maintained that his life was saved by a farthing in his pocket that deflected the bullet. The lucky farthing is still retained by the Harrod family, although his daughter said that because of his injury the only employment open to him was odd-job gardening.

Another casualty, Arthur Robson, who spent many months in hospital prior to his discharge from the army in 1917, suffered from a damaged lung for the rest of his life.

When the War Memorial was dedicated on New Year's Day, 1921, the Bishop of Rochester thanked God for the vision and courage of the young men but also for the heroism of those at home, "who hid an aching heart with a smiling face" — a recognition of the sorrow experienced by so many families.

As a result of the war the village structure altered. There were now twice as many women as men, a situation that only slowly changed in the following decade. Many of the owners of the larger houses had difficulty in getting staff. Heavy taxation in the war had affected their income and in some cases, such as Mr and Mrs Wood at Glebe House, their only son and heir had died. Consequently, they decided to sell up and move away. In many cases the estates were sold to developers and eventually it led to the building boom in Hayes in the 1930s.

The transformation of Hayes from a quiet rural village into a larger community had begun.

Sources

Bromley Archives P180/ 25/11, *Hayes C of E School Log Book*
CWGC, *Debt of Honour Register*
Library and Archive Canada, *Canadian Convalescent Hospital, Bromley*
Plant family papers
Arthur Robson family papers
Chris Timms
Jean Wilson and Trevor Woodman, *Hayes a History of a Kentish Village*, Vol. II, 2012
Hayes in World War I, 1989, Jean Wilson
The Village School, Hayes, 1987, Jean Wilson

Kelsey Manor, Beckenham, *above — the site of today's Kelsey Park — a hospital for wounded soldiers and the headquarters of transport of the Army Service Corps in WWI. The house was demolished in 1921. (PL)*

Oakwood, *below, was another of the grand Beckenham houses that at the end of its days found a new use as a barracks. It survived until the 1930s and its name lives on in Oakwood Avenue (PL)*

Billeted in the Borough

Beckenham to Green Street Green

Christine Hellicar

It was not only wounded soldiers who became a regular sight on the streets of Bromley. Many regiments were based in Kent while they trained and waited for embarkation to France, and large buildings were commandeered as barracks. Bromley, with plenty of open space for training and good train links to the coast, was an ideal spot for billeting large numbers of men.

Soldiers kept in touch with friends and relatives by letter and postcard. A postcard was the quickest and cheapest way to get a message home quickly, often to say the sender had arrived back from leave or would be home next day. With several postal collections and deliveries every day, news travelled fast. Local photographers soon found a ready market for postcards showing the various barracks. Ted, writing to Esher from his billet at Oakwood House, Beckenham, said: *"Will be home tomorrow all being well ... will catch the 2.30 post so you will get this tomorrow."*

Oakwood, now demolished and replaced by a housing estate, was one of the grand houses in Beckenham used by the army. For most of the soldiers these were the kind of properties they would only have ever entered before the war as servants or tradesman.

The view of Oakwood on the opposite page was sent to Warminster by "Your devoted H". The short message captures some of his feelings about the barracks: *"My dearest M, a p/c of entrance to Oakwood where we pass through in evening and early morning when camp and world is sleeping. It takes nearly five minutes to walk up from the gate."*

Nearby Kelsey Manor became a hospital and an Army Service Corps base. It had long since ceased to be a private residence, becoming first a convent and then a school. By the outbreak of war it was owned by a property developer and the grounds had been bought by the Beckenham Council. But it certainly impressed one soldier from North Tyne. The message on his card

Barracks in a brewery

The tiny village of Green Street Green had nearly as many soldiers as inhabitants when the old Fox's Brewery became a barracks. Several different regiments were based there during the war. Above, a card sent by Billy to Clara in Walthamstow said: "Just a card to show you our 'Mansion'." (PH) Below, soldiers became an everyday sight on the High Street. (CH)

(pictured, top, Page 106) sent in 1917, said: *"This is not such a bad life after all ... I am quite near Crystal Palace can see it out of the window."* The X no doubt marks the young man's room.

One of the most unusual billets must have been at Green Street Green. Fox's Brewery closed in 1909 and during the war a section was used as a factory, making submarine parts. The rest of the brewery became a barracks and several different regiments were billeted there, the men in the brewery buildings and the officers at a nearby house, The Larches.

They trained at the Glentrammon Recreation Ground, where dugout trenches were made for instructing the troops in field engineering and bombing. At the bottom of nearby Shire Lane there was a rifle range.

Residents recalled *Come to the Cookhouse Boys* being sounded by a bugler and seeing the soldiers lining up at the bottom of Laxey Road (opposite the brewery) with their mugs and plates to collect their meals. Women in the village earned a bit of extra money by washing the shirts of the army officers.

In an attempt to relieve the monotony for the soldiers, the local school and churches organised social occasions and the Sunday school room of the Baptist church at the bottom of Worlds End Lane was used by the men for recreation on weekday evenings. Football matches were played on the former brewery cricket ground and a sports day was organised for the troops.

When the troops left the barracks for France, the school band from nearby St Joseph's Orphanage played as they steamed out of the station at Orpington.

At the beginning of November 1918 the Poplar and Stepney Rifles moved into the barracks and their band was able to celebrate the Armistice by entertaining a crowd of patients from Orpington Hospital gathered in the main road of the hospital.

Green Street Green Baptist Church was one of many churches and voluntary organisations that tried to make life a little brighter for the soldiers billeted or convalescing in the borough. Many ran Soldiers' Clubs. The club at Bromley Congregational Church was one of the biggest. It opened 12 hours a day, seven days a week and was run as a business providing 3,580 meals a week, lectures,

Bromley Congregational Church Soldiers' Club: volunteers, left, not only prepared meals for the soldiers in the club but also knitted garments and sent letters to the men at the front. They also provided clothes for the poor of London during the early part of the war and in 1914 helped Belgian refugees fleeing to England. Below, the lecture hall had two small billiard tables and accommodation for 100 letter writers — stationery provided. The church was on the site of the United Reformed Church next to Boots in Widmore Road. It was destroyed during an air raid in WWII. (BLSL)

professional concerts, classrooms, billiard tables and an area for letter writing.

The church's war history tells us: "They came in thousands for a meal, a smoke, a wash, games, reading, conversation, music and letter writing ... the conditions in which men found themselves on joining up were so unusual, and often so discouraging that they greatly appreciated a club which was warm, comfortable and wholesome, with a minimum of orders, regulations and restrictions."

It added that many of the soldiers' billets, in converted big houses and industrial buildings, had very limited facilities: "Arrangements were made for them [the soldiers] to enjoy the luxury of warm baths in the houses of kind friends in the neighbourhood: for the washing of their clothes, which were mended by ladies before being returned."

HMS Crystal Palace

The strangest change of use for any building in the borough into a military establishment was the Crystal Palace. All the building's artefacts were boxed up and the grounds closed to the public. The Admiralty and the YMCA moved in and it became Royal Naval Shore Station HMS Victory VI — soon known as "HMS Crystal Palace".

Much of the exhibition building and many of the 1911 Festival of Empire buildings in the grounds — pavilions representing different countries — were taken over as offices or billets and for training naval recruits. The Palace itself housed 10,000 men, with sufficient mess accommodation to feed them all at once, and enough "shower fitted baths" for 1,400 men to wash in an hour. Once initial training was completed the men transferred to Blandford, Dorset, still not on the coast but a bit nearer the sea.

Crystal Palace was considered to be a "healthful place for training" according to a *Kentish Times* report in 1915. There were six battalions, of 1,100 men, each treated as separate ships. "The life is that of a huge ship. All men passing the Admiral's flag in the centre of the grounds salute it as they would the flag on a quarter-deck ... looking over the spacious grounds from the terraces, the spectacle of squads of men marching, drilling or engaged in Swedish exercises was as impressive as it was strange."

Some 125,000 men and women trained there and saw action during the 1914 defence of Antwerp, the 1915-16 Gallipoli campaign and extensive battles on the Western Front from 1916 to 1918, when the War Office renamed them the 63rd (RN) Division.

Sources

The Story of Green Street Green School by Patricia Holmes
The Story of Green Street Green Marjorie Ford and Geoffrey Rickard
Orpington Hospital War Diaries
District Times 11 June 1915 and 4 October 1918
A Short History of Our War Work, Bromley Congregational Church
Additional research by Paul Rason, Cliff Watkins and David Johnson

HMS Crystal Palace *chess club was one of the recreational facilities organised for the men billeted in the Palace precincts, a distraction from the nearby public houses. The YMCA organised recreational facilities and the one civilian, seen on the left of the picture — who did not have to wear a hat for the picture — was probably Mr Hodgson of Penge YMCA (DJ)*

A Haven from War

Belgian Refugees 1914

Despite their own hardships and sorrows, the people of Britain opened their doors to thousands of Belgian refugees who had been driven from their homes when the Germans marched into Belgium in 1914.

Three hundred were given a safe haven in the towns and villages of Bromley. One of these was Alfons Selleslagh, who arrived in Bromley in May 1915 with his wife Clémentine and daughter Céline. He had fled Belgium in October 1914 and went first to Alexandra Palace, one of the major reception centres for Belgian refugees, then, for a short time, to Burton-on-Trent. By 1915 the family had made their wartime home at 19 Palace Grove, Bromley.

Why they ended up in Bromley is not known, but many church and community organisations in Bromley were offering to help via the national War Refugees Committee or their own networks. The Selleslagh family came from the small village of Humbeek, Brabant. Their great-grandson, Frans Van Humbeek, takes up their story: "In our otherwise quiet village ordinary people were taken hostage, the priest of the neighbouring village was tortured and brutally murdered, the Germans burned down several streets of houses, they burned down the church of Humbeek and other churches in the region."

From postcards of Bromley sent by Alfons — which were censored so do not give a lot of information — and from the Belgian National Archives, Frans has pieced together a little of his family's time in Bromley. Like all refugees, Alfons, then 48, had to register with the police, which he did in June 1915. He found work as a timberman with Boardman Timber Merchants in Tweedy Road, Bromley, but is believed to have been working later for the Sheaf family, timber merchants in Southlands Road. Clémentine and Céline probably worked as dressmakers. It was the first time they had left Belgium and they spoke only Dutch. The Selleslagh

The Selleslagh family, *pictured left, were among 300 Belgian refugees given shelter and friendship in Bromley. (FVH)*
Many *local people in Beckenham joined the refugees to celebrate Belgische nationale feestdag on 21 July 1916, pictured below (PL). The celebrations marked the start of the independent state of Belgium in 1831 under a constitutional monarchy and parliament.*

family returned home to Belgium on 23 October 1919.

The people of Bromley did a great deal to make the Belgian refugees welcome and among the places the Selleslagh family may have visited was the Bromley Congregational Church. In its history of the war it sets the scene: "August–September 1914. Then began the immense tragic flight of the inhabitants of Belgium ... crowding aboard the ships, without food, without clothing, until there was not even standing room on the decks." More than 25,000 buildings had been destroyed by arson — not in battle — when the Germans marched into Belgium. By early October, 200,000 refugees were in a Britain not prepared for such an influx.

Nationally a War Refugees Committee was set up and the Government announced that it would offer "victims of war the hospitality of the British nation". This national response to the tragedy was matched by the work of local organisations. Alongside its work for soldiers billeted in Bromley, the Bromley Congregational Church arranged housing, furniture, clothing and schooling for the refugee families. There were classes in English and help was given for them to find work and independence.

The hand of friendship was offered in other ways. A report in the *Bromley and District Times* on 13 November 1914 told of the, "universal desire to do something for the brave Belgian soldiers and the Belgian refugees around the town". A concert had been arranged for them at Hayes School with the children singing several national anthems — including the Japanese — and the audience joined in with Auld Lang Syne, which was "participated in with interest by the Belgians". Such entertainments for refugees, troops and injured soldiers were a regular part of wartime life.

The Selleslagh family's welcome must have been very warm, for in 1945 members of the Sheaf family went to Belgium from their home at 63 Victoria Road, Bromley, for the marriage of Céline's daughter, who was the mother of Frans Van Humbeek.

Sources Frans Van Humbeek
Fighting on the Home Front, The Legacy of Women in World War One,
Kate Adie; Bromley Congregational Church WWI history

The Ontario Military Hospital at Orpington was
opened on 16 February 1916 by the Secretary of State
for the Colonies, Andrew Bonar Law. It was a cold, wet,
gloomy day with mud everywhere, but the local paper
reported that this failed to dampen the enthusiasm of
those present or to spoil the splendour of what was a
great local event.

The buildings were huts constructed of timber and
asbestos on low brick walls and were meant to last for
the duration of the war. However, they were to remain
an integral part of the Orpington scene for more than
60 years. (OHO)

Ontario's Generous Gift
Orpington 1916 – 1919
Christine Hellicar

"As a war gift to the motherland it is unique. Founded as Ontario's tribute to the war it has been foremost in every development of the healing art under war conditions ... Orpington has stood unrivalled as an overseas hospital."
— 1919 Canadian report on the military hospital

When 107 wounded soldiers, mainly Canadians, New Zealanders and Australians arrived at Orpington Station on 8 June 1916 they were not destined for one of the VAD hospitals but were the first patients for what was to become the 16th Canadian General (Ontario) Hospital, known locally as the Ontario Hospital.

It was a 1,000-bed "state-of-the-art" facility built in just four months. Soon, plans were afoot for enlargement and by July 1917 there were over 2,000 beds. It closed in May 1919 and in that time staff had cared for 30,294 men — more than 12,000 from Britain, 16,402 from Canada and the rest from Australia, New Zealand and elsewhere. It took the most serious cases: 80% were shrapnel and high explosive bullet wounds and patients suffering "nerve injuries". It did pioneering work in facial surgery.

The Canadians were immensely proud of the hospital. It was one of the largest and most up-to-date in the world and it was paid for from the $2 million (£400,000) war relief fund that had been set up by the Government of Ontario shortly after the outbreak of the war.

It was not just the country's top doctors and 200 state registered graduate nurses who staffed the hospital. One visitor was told by the quartermaster: "Unless you are a good citizen of Ontario you can't get a job on this place." There were more than 1,000 doctors, nurses, officers and men running the hospital and in charge throughout the war was Colonel DW McPherson, a doctor with a civilian practice in Toronto. He had been a member of the Canadian Militia before the war and had already served in France.

There were 52-bed wards with special rooms for the seriously ill, an isolation unit, X-ray departments, kitchens, a chapel, a post office, recreation rooms, a concert hall, a book store, canteen, a barbers and it even had its own generators and central heating. The operating theatres were, "fitted with every appliance for the amelioration of suffering and for efficiency". By the end of January 1919 there had been 3,392 operations.

Visitors also noted the specialist staff such as Dietician Miss McAdams — a role almost unknown in Britain at that time — who had oversight of the preparation of all the food from a scientific point of view.

The visitor, Gertrude Vaughan, recorded in *The World's Work* magazine: "The mere fact that the curtains for the hundreds of windows cost something like £1,500 indicates the scale on which they do things at Orpington. There must be miles of linoleum, and one might almost say that a small forest went into the making of the wooden portions of the huts themselves. With hardly an exception the whole of the outfit has been sent over from Ontario, and we passed on our rounds bales upon bales — all coming direct or through the Canadian Red Cross in London — of comforts, as well as medical and surgical necessaries for the patients.

"The huts are built of asbestos and are as nearly fire-proof as possible. All are painted green in the interior, and the effect of this, with the brown woodwork, is particularly pleasing and restful."

The Ontario Hospital attracted a lot of attention. It had been officially opened in February 1916 by Andrew Bonar Law, the Secretary of State for the Colonies, who had been born in Canada. In its three years of operation it had a flow of distinguished visitors — bishops, dukes, the Prime Ministers of Ontario and Canada. In March 1919 King George and Queen Mary paid a private visit.

The hospital war diaries record: "They were very impressed by the equipment. His Majesty especially commented on the brightness and cheerful appearance and airiness of the wards."

The Royal couple chatted to patients and took tea with the nurses.

They were not the first to be impressed. In the *District Times* in July 1916 a reporter commented: "It was an additional pleasure to go over this up-to-date hospital, a marvel of medical science."

He was reporting on a Dominion Day baseball match between The Ontario and the Canadian Convalescent House at Uxbridge. He commented: "It was easy to judge from the outspoken comments on the game and the quaint cries of encouragement they were from Canada's fair domain." Another visitor commented: "How strange the Canadian intonation sounds."

The report notes that "a number of civilians" had been invited to attend the event and that the band of St Joseph's Orphanage, which was just across Sevenoaks Road from the hospital, played. This orphanage had strong links with Ontario. For 25 years boys from the school were sent to New Orpington Lodge, a Canadian home in Ottawa. Many of them returned as part of the Canadian Expeditionary Force and some found themselves back in Orpington as patients.

However, it was not this old link that brought the Canadians to Orpington but practical considerations. In the summer of 1915 William Hearst, the Prime Minister of Ontario, announced that they wanted to build a hospital to "help the Motherland". Nearly half the Canadian soldiers who enlisted for the war came from Ontario and when wounded found themselves scattered in different hospitals "lacking the companionship of their comrades". A hospital, the Ontario Government decided, was the most useful gift to help both soldiers and Britain.

Several sites were looked at with the priorities being proximity to a railway line, abundant fresh water, good sewerage and quiet and restful surroundings. A post-war report to the Canadian government records: "The surroundings of the hospital are of the most delightful character. Nothing could surpass the quiet beauty of this green and well-wooded countryside."

The Ontario Government settled on leasing 70 acres of The Boundary Estate, Orpington. The hospital cost $475,000 to build, $187,028 for equipment and $150,000 a year to run and the land was to be given back to the owner six months after the end of the

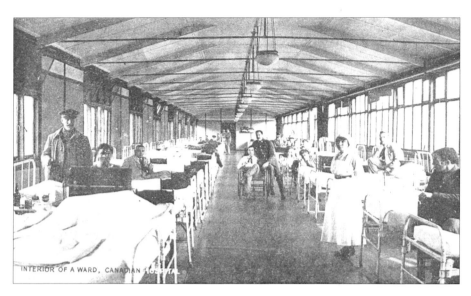

INTERIOR OF A WARD, CANADIAN HOSPITAL

The wards, above, in the Ontario Hospital were clean, light and airy and provided every modern facility available for medical care. Below, the road into the site with the "huts", left, that were to serve the people of Orpington for over 60 years as part of the local hospital.

war "in the condition in which it was taken over". The biggest headache for the builders was "the scarcity of material and labour". But not as much as a headache as the construction caused local farmers. With labour already short, the high wages paid by the Canadians to building labourers, 6d an hour, was nearly double the minimum paid to agricultural workers.

But once up and running the Ontario Hospital was taken under the wing of the local community, who were already providing support for soldiers in the VAD hospitals — including the local Village Hall VAD hospital — and Belgian refugees. The population of the village would have risen by half when the hospital was fully operational and around the district the Dominion men and women were an unusual sight. Gertrude Vaughan wrote: "Everywhere one meets them, swinging along at an easy stride or dashing past in cars or going more slowly in the ambulances which are part of the munificent equipment sent over to the Mother Country by her sons and daughters on 'the other side'."

These must have been the staff. What she did not see, or did not mention, were the visitors to the Soldiers' Club at Orpington Baptist Church over a mile away. A report on the club activities paints a graphic picture: "Every afternoon a pilgrimage took place between the Ontario Military Hospital and the Club. It was a pathetic sight, this procession of the maimed and halt, on crutches, in wheeled chairs and carriages, leaning on sticks or on a friendly comrade's arm, bearing in their bodies the sign manual of the sacrifices they had made to serve the Empire in her need."

The hospital war diaries show that regular visits were arranged for soldiers and medical staff to some of the more substantial homes across the borough while for those who could walk, district tea parties were given by local residents.

Concert parties came from London and local schools and orchestral societies entertained the wounded. The Ladies' Work Association taught the recovering men a range of sedentary skills from Old English embroidery, knitting and sewing to wood carving and bead work. There was a rota of lady hospital visitors. They brought flowers and sympathy, while their menfolk were more likely to join in the sporting activities. Sports on Dominion Day would "not easily pass from the memories of those who participated in them", according to a 1919 history of the hospital.

Everyone wanted to help. For a short time in 1916 the hospital had its own newspaper, *The Ontario Stretcher*, printed by Bromley and West Kent Newspapers, and internationally-renowned local poultry farmer William Cook gave the hospital three Buff Orpington prize hens as mascots. They had "a special little house in the grounds".

Local businessman Albert Spencer May, who owned the Orpington Picture Palace, showed films in the hospital recreation room twice a week. The more able men also visited the Palace — known locally as "the Bug Hutch" — and to reassure the soldiers programmes issued during the war carried a note informing patrons that the cinema had an early warning alarm system in the event of air raids. The "system" was a group of plane and airship spotters who would signal by means of flags from distances as far as Polhill. This was to give reassurance to those troops who were suffering from "shell shock" after serving in the front-line in France. Though what should happen in the event of such a warning was not stated on the programme.

The planes did come in 1917 and batteries of anti-aircraft guns and large numbers of searchlights were installed in the district. People watched the planes and heard the gunfights above as the German Gothas headed for London and reported seeing the flames as two Zeppelins were brought down nearer the city. But the closest the war came to Orpington was when an aerial torpedo fell on an orchard and stripped a number of apple trees. The following morning the apples were collected and two days later sold at Covent Garden.

A post-war history written by the Workers Educational Association (WEA) records that by September 1917 the noise was "voted a nuisance, but in general the village took the air raids very quietly". What was probably more unsettling, especially for the "nerve injury" patients at the Ontario Hospital, was the sound of the guns on the Western Front.

The distance from Orpington to Ypres as the crow flies is 120 miles. "Throughout [the war] the sound of the guns in Flanders was heard in Orpington over extended periods of time ... for most part the impression given was of a continuous series of dull thuds punctuated at intervals by periods of greater or lesser intensity. The firing was audible by day as well as by night and on some occasions it continued for several weeks without intermission. Not infrequently the sound was sufficiently intense to be disturbing and to cause windows to rattle."

While everyone was trying to make life for the soldiers a little brighter, the hospital authorities had to contend with a constant turnover of staff with medical officers, nurses and staff leaving daily for France, and some very complex medical cases. Gertrude Vaughan noted: "Mental cases are alas a common occurrence." A WEA visitor recorded: "There are continuous baths for nerve, shell shock and multiple wounds ... No 17 ward is for paraphegia

Still a small village, Orpington's population of 6,000 was swelled by an additional 3,000 when the Ontario Hospital opened. These Elizabethan cottages stood on the High Street near the present covered entrance to The Walnuts.

The Canadians described Orpington as "a quiet peaceful village ... [it] still retains its rural charm and has many picturesque cottages and old houses dating back to Tudor times ... the surroundings of the hospital are of the most delightful character". (CH)

[impairment in motor or sensory function to the lower limbs] cases, No 18 for tubercular suspects, No 19 chest cases, No 20 tubercular."

Then there was Major Le Sueur's studio, known as "the beauty parlour", where he made plaster casts of jaws and faces to help with the reconstruction of facial wounds. Captain Duff invented painted fingers and spectacles with the eye painted on them for when no socket remained for an artificial eye, and in the dental clinic they provided artificial jaws, teeth and artificial bridges. This was pioneering work which fed into that being done in the same field at Queen Mary's Hospital in Sidcup.

As the war drew to an end and into 1919 the hospital war diaries record a new problem — influenza hitting both patients and medical staff. In November 1918, alongside the thanksgiving party and a visit of the 17th London Regimental Band, then stationed at nearby Green Street Green, the diary records 29 sisters sick and all leave cancelled.

The buildings officially ceased to be the Canadian Military Hospital on 20 September 1919. But nine days before that, the hospital experienced a joyous event. The pregnant wife of Sergeant Dahl of the Canadian Army was visiting her husband, who was about to leave for

Soldiers gathered outside the hospital and, in the background, the clock which was part of the reception block. It is pictured, right in 2014, now in the hospital's courtyard garden. It has been preserved and renovated by the Friends of Orpington Hospital. (OHO andCH)

Canada on the hospital ship *Araguaya,* when she went into labour. Leslie Jack Dahl was born a few hours later and the war diary notes they were both doing well.

Post Script

Orpington will never forget the Canadians. In "Canadian Corner" at All Saints Church 116 men who breathed their last at the Ontario Hospital lie buried in a Commonwealth War Graves Commission site: 88 Canadians, five Australians and 23 UK soldiers. Eleven of the Canadians and one of the Australians had been born in the UK.

In memory of those men the Workers' Educational Association produced a book about the history of Orpington entitled *From Saxon Times to The Great War* and sent a copy to the family of every man who lies in the churchyard. In a covering letter they said: *"We wish you to feel that friendly hands will tend his grave, and that kindly hearts reverence his memory and sympathise with you in your sorrow."*

The land did not return to The Boundary Estate. The hospital remained, sold to the Ministry of Pensions for £80,000. It eventually became part of the NHS, and still is. Those state-of-the-art buildings — known locally in later years as "the huts" — lasted for 63 years. The last few were demolished in the early 1980s. Much smaller now, Orpington Hospital is part of the King's College Hospital NHS Foundation Trust. In the entrance area a mural commissioned in 2009 commemorates the hospital's beginnings but all that remains of the original buildings is the clock tower.

Sources *Ontario Military Hospital, Orpington, Kent,* historical report prepared for GH Ferguson, Minister of Lands, Forests and Mines, Ontario, Canada, 1919

The World's Work Magazine, July 1916

Ontario Archives online, war diaries ,Canadian Great War project online

Orpington Hospital Canadian History Project Mural, project report

Orpington from Saxon Times to The Great War, WEA history, 1919

Letters of George Miller

The Ontario Stretcher, 1916

District Times, 1916, *Canadian Corner, a brief history* John Pateman

A Defence Fledgling
Biggin Hill

Biggin Hill is the most iconic wartime site in Bromley but its role in defending Britain was only just taking off in World War One. In 1914 the area was little more than a farm, a mansion called Aperfield Court and a few scattered houses on the road from Keston to Westerham.

But the flat open space of Biggin Hill, atop one of the highest points in Kent, had already caught the eye of early aviators when in 1912 a pilot from the Royal Flying Corps, flying over the Weald of Kent, experienced engine trouble.

"To his delight he saw before him a long straight high plateau, standing proud from the land all around it. He felt that this was an ideal spot [for an emergency landing] and he gently brought his aircraft to the ground," Josie Cole says in her article in the *Beckenham Historian* How Biggin Hill Aerodrome Began.

Subsequently the pilot reported to his superiors that he had found an ideal emergency landing strip and within weeks the War Office had come to an agreement with the tenant farmer and the land owner, Earl Stanhope, to lease the field.

When war broke out the field was used for emergency night landings but in 1915 it took on a new role. Wireless testing was taking place at Joyce Green Testing Park in Dartford. It was only just above sea level and fog, mists and poor wireless reception made it very unsuitable.

One of the experts working at Dartford was Lieutenant Furnival who lived in Limpsfield, near Biggin Hill. "He realised what a suitable site Biggin Hill would be as it is more than 700 feet above sea-level," says Josie Cole.

Within weeks, in the autumn of 1916, plans were made to turn Biggin Hill into a Wireless Testing Park and by the winter it was a tented city with canvas hangars. In 1917 Aperfield Court, with its spacious grounds, was requisitioned and a powerful wireless transmitter installed for ground control of fighter aeroplanes that were defending London. Another house, Koonowla, a children's home, became the officers' mess.

> **The winter of 1917 was extremely cold. On 2 January when the first plane landed for wireless experimentation it had snowed heavily. When the pilot and engineer emerged from the plane they were bombarded with snowballs.**

In February 1917 the area was officially named Biggin Hill Aerodrome and work continued on developing the wireless. Within a short time they were able to send messages from a transmitter on the ground and give pilots instructions. Because of the success, all manufacturing of the radios was transferred to Biggin Hill and The Wireless Experimental Establishment was set up.

Biggin Hill became a school for wireless telephony in aeroplanes, with 36 officers a week passing through the station. Their work was considered so important that King George V was given a demonstration of planes being passed instructions from the ground by a transmitter.

But Biggin Hill was on the flight route of the German Gotha bombers, which were carrying out the first air raids on London. Defence of the aerodrome became crucial. In 1918 the first squadron to be stationed there was a detachment of the 39th squadron and from this was formed a new squadron, 141.

And so, as the war ended, the makeshift aerodrome for testing wireless began to change and 18 months after canvas tents and hangers had first been erected, building work began in earnest to create the Biggin Hill that was to play such a crucial part in the next war.

Sources
How Biggin Hill Aerodrome Began, Josie Cole, Beckenham Historian April 2013
Articles in *Bromleage* 1976, *Bromleag* 2006

Parades, *such as this one through Bromley High Street, were organised to mark the end of the war but although there are crowds the mood here is sombre, with no flag waving and a stillness about the spectators. This picture was taken as the march passed The Bell public house on the far right. (MR)*

Peace for a Time

Max Batten

"The Dawn: The greatest day of all days has just dawned for England and her Allies ... the objects for which Britain entered the war have been achieved ... and a regenerated civilisation, free from the hearty fear of war will arise from the terrible holocaust."
— Editorial in the Bromley and District Times 16 November 1918

The Armistice was signed at 5am on Monday 11 November 1918 and the ceasefire was to come into force at 11am. For some, the information only came with newspapers published at midday, but for many the news had spread from workers returning in lorries from Biggin Hill carrying "The Victory RAF" on their sides.

At 11 o'clock, large guns and a succession of maroons were fired. People put out flags of all shapes and sizes and of many nations. In Bromley Post Office staff stopped work briefly to join in the singing and the Parish Church bells were rung — but to little effect as they were surrounded by protective shutters, thanks to DORA. (See Page 57) The Education Committee seemed unaffected, insisting children remain in school until the usual time, although children in Beckenham were more fortunate, getting the afternoon off, as did council staff.

And yet, in the spring of 1918, a successful German offensive had made this all look very unlikely. But on 4 August there was a Grand Demonstration on Martin's Hill in Bromley, led by the Mayor Councillor Fred Gillett JP, HW Forster MP, Sir Thomas Dewey, Coles Child and other local dignitaries. The words of King George V, who was confident there was some expectation that "a victorious peace was not far distant", were read to a cheering crowd followed by patriotic speeches and tributes to the fallen. Nevertheless, even by October, it still seemed uncertain that war could end before Christmas.

So, although some whispers of peace began on Thursday 7 November, the local paper the next day looked much as usual, reduced to eight pages by paper shortages, with advert No 13 on how to save money — for example, carry home your own parcels, and use the money saved to invest in War Savings Certificates (£1 bond for 15s-6d [77½p], £500 for £387-10s). Another advert headed "A coal poker is a coal waster" exhorted people to maximise the use of fuel. Adverts for "Tonic for Shell Shock" and a surgical-boot maker (military/navel orders given priority) were also a sign of the times.

The Bromley Tribunal listed men, mostly from shops or offering services like undertaking and chimney sweeping, who were given a three-month extension to their exemption from military service. But this time the list was headed "The Last Sitting?" Talk of National Reconstruction was in the air and the need to find employment for millions of men and women as the war ended was being discussed. It was also a topic for a conference of the Bromley and Shortlands branch of the Women's Total Abstinence Union on 31 October.

It seemed to be business as usual in the courts, however, with drunk and disorderly conduct and an unlucky resident of Sandford Road, Bromley, who was fined nine shillings (45p) for having no lights on her bicycle. But there *were* differences, with deserters being charged and several cases of misbehaving children and the illegal employment of young children highlighting the effects of missing fathers and labour shortages. A Penge baker was fined for selling bread *less* than 12 hours old and two men were summoned for using petrol without authority in Beckenham, namely carrying guests from a wedding to a reception!

Bromley Council were also concerned about wasting fuel and the amount of poorly burned ash they were collecting. A complaint about some road menders was investigated but found to be baseless: they had in fact been using the tar-heating machine economically to cook their lunches. Suggestions that street lighting could be restored were rejected, at least for a week or two.

Obituaries, often headed "For King and Country", of soldiers and sailors appeared in every paper — as they had done throughout the war — along with messages from bereaved families thanking friends and neighbours for their comfort at a time of great loss. But there was also a new threat — influenza. Although it was under-reported, it was clear that an increasing number of people were suffering from a virulent strain of the virus and, in too many cases, suffering complications such as pneumonia which led to their death. Unusually, the disease particularly affected people aged between 20 and 40 and cases were arising of young wives dying while their husbands survived at the Front. An advert for Jeyes' Fluid promoted its protective properties against flu.

A week later, it all looked different. A large advert for a "Victory Week" carpet sale led the way, with Bromley Patriotic Concerts under Miss Gwynne Kimpton planning a *Victory and the Coming of Peace* celebration at the Central Hall on 30 November. Two soldiers were to address a Patriotic Meeting in the Village Hall in Chislehurst on the 21st.

Services of thanksgiving were held in many churches that first evening with many more-formal ones the following Sunday. The Mayor raised the question of a memorial in Bromley and invited contributions. Appeals were made for money and clothes in aid of Belgian relief. Belgium had suffered more than any other country in the conflict. On Tuesday 12th, boys from the County School in Hayes Lane arranged an evening march with banners and torch bearers, drums and bugles while Beckenham school children organised a grand firework display. Despite DORA, shades were removed from street lights as normality began to return.

Electioneering began in earnest for the first General Election to be held on a single day, 14 December, and by 23 November the Beckenham Food Control Department revealed that over Christmas meat rations would be doubled and turkey would be unrestricted. But, despite the celebrations and relief, many families were grieving for lost ones and dire warnings of continuing shortages to come still filled many column inches.

Sources *Bromley and District Times* 10 August, 15 and 22 November 1918
Beckenham Journal/Penge and Sydenham Advertiser 9, 16 and 23 November 1918;
Chislehurst and District Times 15 and 22 November 1918;
Wikipedia

One of the most striking memorials in the borough is to the 769 men of Bromley town who lost their lives. It stands near the Parish Church at the top of Martin's Hill. Designed and sculpted by Sydney March, it is listed by English Heritage as a Grade II* structure.

Sydney was one of the March family whose studios were in Farnborough at Goddendene, which stood on the site now occupied by Sainsbury's. They sculptured national War Memorials throughout the world.

It was unveiled on 29 October 1922 by Lord Henry Horne, a WWI general, and dedicated by the Bishop of Rochester, John Harmer. (CH)

Preserving the War Memorials

The disappearance of war memorials has been a concern since the 1980s so the Imperial War Museum (IWM) began building a database listing all the memorials in the UK.

It started as a project to gather details of The Great War memorials but was extended to include all conflicts because of the loss of many through vandalism, theft, neglect and, sadly, indifference. Others were disappearing as buildings, in particular religious buildings, were made redundant or demolished.

Leading up to the millennium, research was carried out in Bromley and a detailed report was produced and included in the IWM database. More than 300 memorials were recorded within the borough, ranging in time from the South African (Boer) War to Korea in 1950 and Malaya 1951, naming the many individuals who lost their lives in the course of their duties. Some memorials name just one man while others name all who came from a parish or town or as members of sports clubs etc.

Paul Rason, who carried out much of the Bromley research, has commented: "A memorial in some cases is the actual building or it is built into the fabric, which admittedly, can be difficult to detach or reinstate if the building is to be pulled down. Often memorials are saved, as indeed many historic buildings are saved, by the efforts of a small group determined to keep these aspects of our communal history, but, sadly again, the drive to save money and do away with the old moves quicker in many cases, so many are lost."

The eventual work was produced in five volumes, giving details of each memorial and a map of its location and in most case a photograph. These volumes are held now in the Local Studies Library of the Central Library in Bromley. A complete set was lodged with the Imperial War Museum.

Sources Guide

WWI material held at Bromley Local Studies and Archives

Francesca Mould

This abridged guide is an introduction to the material held at Bromley Local Studies and Archives for those researching First World War Bromley. It covers the period 1914 – 1920.

It was compiled as part of Bromley Local Studies Heritage Lottery Funded Project "Caring for the Casualties of the First World War in Bromley" June 2014.

The full guide is available at: www.bromleyfirstworldwar.org.uk

Local Studies material — *open access*

Newspaper titles

Beckenham & Penge Advertiser
Beckenham Journal Beckenham & District Times
Bromley Chronicle
Bromley & District Times
Bromley Local Guide and Advertiser
Chislehurst & District Times
Penge & Anerley Express
St Mary Cray Orpington & District Times
Sidcup & District Times
St Mary Cray & Swanley Express & North Kent Observer
continued as St Mary Cray & Swanley Express
Orpington Express & North Kent Observer
Sydenham & Penge Gazette

Local Studies photographic collection

The photographic collection contains more than 17,000 photographs in the form of scans, prints, slides, lantern slides and negatives. There is an index that notes whether the photograph is in colour or black and white, the print size, area, building name and road, description, dates, format and notes.

Photos covering the First World War period include those of schools used as military hospitals, Voluntary Aid Detachment (VAD) hospitals, staff of VAD hospitals, images of the Canadian Convalescent Hospital, war memorials, men setting off to enlist or leaving for the front.

Additional image collections
— *not open access**

There are a number of image collections within the archives collection. Two collections of note are those of Joyce Walker and George

Early Morning in the Ward.

William Smith, both of which show the activities of the Red Cross and the VADs in Bromley during WWI.

Street directories contain introductions to areas giving historical background, information on what is going on at the time and advertisements, as well as lists of residents arranged by street, businesses and tradespeople.

Each parish has a separate entry. Some directories contain a diary of the year or visitor guides and local information, postal arrangements, pensions, tax, insurance and a summary of the Registration Act.

Electoral rolls list the people registered to vote of an area. The lists are arranged by parliamentary district and by road name. It was only in 1918 that all men aged 21 or over and women over the age of 30 who were married, had property or were a graduate in a university constituency, could vote.

Registration was suspended during the First World War and so no registers exist for 1916 and 1917 and coverage for some constituencies prior to and immediately after the war is not complete. In 1918, a general election year, an absent voters list was produced which gave details of men aged over 21 who were in the armed forces.

Council minutes are the written records of discussions and proceedings of council meetings. The minutes can give a sense of the issues that affected the area and how the council responded.

We hold minutes for the First World War period for the following councils: Bromley Borough Council, Beckenham District Council, Urban District Council of Penge, Bromley Rural District Council, Chislehurst Urban District and for Chelsfield, Farnborough, Knockholt, Mottingham and St Paul's Cray parish councils. For Orpington and West Wickham there are some minutes, but not full coverage of the WWI period. We do not hold minutes for Cudham, Downe or Keston.

Archives Material — *not open access**

The collection encompasses parish records, school records and workhouse records as well as estate papers, business papers and personal papers.

Parish records held include baptism registers, marriage registers, burial registers, parish meeting minutes and, for a few parishes, parish magazines.

School records include admissions registers, logbooks, staff registers and publications.**

Logbooks are the permanent records kept by the headmaster or headmistress logging the events and proceedings that affected and shaped the school each school week.

The entries can cover anything from school organisation, arrangements, the introduction of new books or apparatus, examinations, courses of instruction, reports by inspectors, visits, absence, illness and special circumstances. They record when the school year commenced, when and why a school would close, the variations in attendance and any deviations from the ordinary running of the school.

Additionally, a logbook holds the record of how the school celebrated special days — for example, Armistice Day and Ascension Day. For the most part, the entries are concise and are what the head teacher would have felt deserved to be recorded.

Staff registers give the names of members of staff and personal details including their qualifications. For the war years they tell us which members of staff enlisted and whether they returned or not.

Admission registers give names and some personal details but unlike the staff registers they do not help to identify those pupils who joined up for the military during the First World War, since most people were only at school until they were 12 or 14 years old. They can show up children who were refugees through the "last school attended" column.

Workhouse records are held for the Bromley Union workhouse at Locksbottom, Farnborough. The parishes the union covered included: Bromley, Beckenham, Chelsfield, Chislehurst, Foots Cray, North Cray, St Mary Cray, St Paul's Cray, Cudham, Downe, Farnborough, Hayes, Keston, Knockholt, Orpington and West Wickham.

The records consist of the Creed Registers, which record the religious creeds of the inmates in the workhouse, birth and death registers and letters from the workhouse to the Local Government Board. These can give more details of inmates and of workhouse staff.

Rolls of Honour confirm, list and honour the names of those who served and lost their lives in the First World War. Rolls of honour can be compiled for a particular church, town, village, workplace, club, school and so on.

These records have to be retrieved from the archive store by a member of the Bromley Local Studies staff. Users need to be members of Bromley Libraries, but membership is free. It is best to order them before going to the library.
**Some records within these collections are subject to statutory closures. Please contact Local Studies for further clarification.*

Bromley Local Studies Library is based at the Central Library, High Street, Bromley, BR1 1EX
www.bromley.gov.uk

BBLHS Publications

In and Around Bromley at the Turn of the Century
Change was in the air in 1900, spreading out from the
growing metropolis. Invention, suburbia and growing
population affected every aspect of life. This book looks
at life in 15 different parts of the borough ranging from
the town of Bromley to the tiny village of Downe.

The Town of Bromley A Century Ago
An in-depth look at life in the largest and busiest of
the borough's urban areas, Bromley town. Each
chapter focuses on a different aspect of life, including
transport, health and leisure at the end of the 19th
century.

Industry and Enterprise
Percy Cox's steam bicycle, a famous Victorian baby
food manufacturer, an aircraft factory, an innovative
department store owner, brewers and paper mills have
been among the industries that have shaped Bromley
borough's past. This book explores these and many
more fascinating aspects of our industrial heritage.

West Wickham Fields and Farmers
Patricia Knowlden
Centuries of change in one small village are explored
through the history of the eight main farms of West
Wickham. The book also contains nine walks — with
maps — around this still-rural and often unchanged
landscape.

For more information contact: admin@bblhs.org.uk